Praise for *Lovi*

"Going from a brief, sophisticated overview of anthropology and philosophy to the down-to-earth reality that pastors, educators, counselors, and parents must confront on transgender issues, this book will prove to be an indispensable resource."

> — *Fr. Robert Sirico*
> *President emeritus and co-founder, The Acton Institute*

"This is, to date, the most comprehensive popular treatment of the Catholic position on gender ideology available. John Bursch has provided an excellent guidebook not only for clergy, teachers, medical specialists, and politicians but also for the average Catholic who is increasingly pressured to conform to this medically, psychologically, and spiritually damaging popular cultural agenda. He has courageously stepped into the breach, producing an intelligent, faithful, and sensitive approach to meet the challenge to either conform to the culture or be branded a hate-promoting bigot. Indispensable."

> — *Fr. Robert J. Spitzer, S.J., Ph.D.*
> *President, Magis Institute of Reason and Faith*
> *Author of* The Moral Wisdom of the Catholic Church

"Many faithful Catholics have a difficult time both understanding and articulating the Church's teachings about the difficult moral and cultural issues of our time. Because they lack confidence and because they fear being canceled or accused of bigotry, they remain silent even with members of their own families. *Loving God's Children: The Church and Gender Ideology* is a wonderfully practical tool to help both laity and clergy to gain the confidence and the vocabulary to articulate the Church's teaching clearly and lovingly. All the important details and applications are covered. I look forward to John Bursch's giving us similar books regarding the other controverted and sensitive moral issues of our time."

> — *+Charles J. Chaput, O.F.M. Cap.*
> *Archbishop Emeritus of Philadelphia*

"Over the past decade, American culture has been overrun by gender ideology — a grave threat not only to the happiness of individuals but also to our very understanding of the person. It is the Catholic Church that provides the clearest and most charitable presentation of the truth of human sexuality, and in so doing, she defends human nature itself. John Bursch's powerful book presents the Church's teaching with clarity and charity. It draws deeply from the Church's wisdom and addresses the most current challenges with authentic compassion. It is an excellent resource for all those — parents and friends, priests and pastors, Catholics and non-Catholics — who find themselves facing this new challenge."

— Very Rev. Paul D. Scalia
Episcopal Vicar for Clergy, Diocese of Arlington

"There are few things more manic and mad than radical relativism's meltdown in the form of gender ideology. What is needed in the midst of such madness is the goodness and truth of the Church's teaching on sexuality and the human body. The sanity and sanctity of such teaching, rooted in reason and love, is laid out with eloquence and lucidity by John Bursch in this excellent and easy-to-read book. We all need to know how to respond with rational love to the madness of gender ideology. This book shows us how to do this. For this reason alone, it should be on every good Catholic's reading list."

— Joseph Pearce
Internationally acclaimed scholar
Author of C. S. Lewis and the Catholic Church *and*
Wisdom and Innocence: A Life of G. K. Chesterton

"The phenomenon of transgenderism discloses a deep suffering that calls for a response of love. John Bursch's book begins from the premise that there is no genuine compassion that is not rooted in truth. Bursch's treatment of Catholic teaching on human love and sexuality and his answers to common practical questions raised by transgenderism offer a valuable orientation to loving in truth — to parents, teachers, and medical professionals who wish to honor the image of God in their children, students, and patients struggling with gender dysphoria."

— Dr. Lesley Rice
Assistant professor of bioethics, Pontifical John Paul II Institute for Studies on
Marriage and Family at the Catholic University of America

"Love is authentic only when grounded in truth. *Loving God's Children* informs readers of the truth — philosophical, theological, scientific, and medical — that they need to know in order to love authentically those caught up in gender ideology. John Bursch has written an accessible and reliable guide for ordinary readers who want to love their neighbors well."

— Ryan T. Anderson, Ph.D.
President, Ethics and Public Policy Center
Author of When Harry Became Sally:
Responding to the Transgender Moment

"The transgender movement has dramatically affected every facet of American life — and Catholics are looking to make sense of it all. I can't think of a wiser guide for that task than attorney and author John Bursch. In his excellent book *Loving God's Children*, Catholics will find answers to questions such as: What is gender ideology? What does the Church teach? How do I love a family member who asserts a "transgender" identity? Writing in a clear, easy style, Bursch draws on Catholic teaching, his extensive legal background, and real-life examples to unpack the truth about who we are and the challenges of gender ideology. This is truly a book that every Catholic adult (and high schooler!) must read!"

— Mary Rice Hasson, J.D.
Director, Person and Identity Project,
Kate O'Beirne Senior Fellow, Ethics and Public Policy Center

LOVING GOD'S CHILDREN

JOHN J. BURSCH

LOVING GOD'S CHILDREN

The Church and Gender Ideology

SOPHIA INSTITUTE PRESS
Manchester, New Hampshire

Cover by Enrique J. Aguilar

Cover image: *Original artwork by Enrique J. Aguilar*

Nihil Obstat:
David S. Crawford, J.D., S.T.D.
Censor Deputatus
May 15, 2023

Imprimatur:
Most Reverend David J. Walkowiak, J.C.D.
Bishop of Grand Rapids
May 19, 2023

Sophia Institute Press
Box 5284, Manchester, NH 03108
1-800-888-9344
www.SophiaInstitute.com

Sophia Institute Press is a registered trademark of Sophia Institute.

paperback ISBN 978-1-64413-936-3

ebook ISBN 978-1-64413-937-0

Library of Congress Control Number: 2023939916

I dedicate this book to my wonderful wife, Angela, and our amazing children. Angela is holy, brilliant, unceasingly patient, and my best friend, and none of my work — including this book — would be possible without her sacrificial love and support, plus her many thoughtful suggestions and contributions. Both she and our children are the best examples of what it means to be courageous and to love others according to God's will. They are a constant inspiration.

Contents

LOVING GOD'S CHILDREN

Introduction

In June 2019, the Catholic Church published an educational document entitled *Male and Female He Created Them: Towards a Path of Dialogue on the Question of Gender Theory in Education*, which outlined certain truths about the human person. The document discussed "the need to educate children and young people to *respect every person* ... so that no one should suffer bullying, violence, insults, or unjust discrimination."[1] But it also compassionately challenged the idea of gender fluidity, and it critiqued the idea that human identity revolves entirely around "the individual's choice" rather than the *"biological difference* between male and female."[2]

The *New York Times* responded almost immediately by publishing an article that said the Church's teaching "encourages hatred,

---

[1] Congregation for Catholic Education, *Male and Female He Created Them: Towards a Path of Dialogue on the Question of Gender Theory in Education* (2019), no. 16; available at http://www.educatio.va/content/dam/cec/Documenti/19_0997_INGLESE.pdf. https://perma.cc/6XHL-M76K

[2] Ibid., no. 22.

bigotry, and violence" against those who identify as transgender.[3] Indeed, the *Times* piece sums up the state of public conversation about gender ideology today: you either agree that sex is defined only by subjective feelings and gross stereotypes about what it means to look and act like a man or woman, or you're someone who encourages hatred, bigotry, and violence.

If this were a mere theoretical discussion, we might just ignore the *Times's* inflammatory language and turn our attention away from the entire debate. We know that Christianity condemns hatred, bigotry, and violence. And we might reasonably ask why it should matter whether a biological man wants to believe he's a woman, a man, both, neither, or something in between. If those types of choices don't harm anyone, shouldn't people be able to believe and live whatever they want?

Why it matters

There are multiple problems with trying to ignore the gender-ideology movement, and we will explore each in detail, and with thorough evidence, in this book.

First, in modern society, gender ideology is pervasive. Everywhere we look, we see trans-identifying individuals in movies, on TV shows, in advertisements — not to mention government directives requiring us to "affirm" those who identify as a gender that is different than their sex. Many people, including celebrities and those in positions of influence, have announced that they identify as one of the many dozens of alternative gender identities; and they insist on being addressed by "preferred pronouns" and titles. Biological males identifying as females are competing in — and winning — athletic

---

[3] Jason Horowitz & Elisabetta Povoledo, "Vatican Rejects Notion That Gender Identity Can Be Fluid," *New York Times,* June 10, 2019, https://www.nytimes.com/2019/06/10/world/europe/vatican-francis-gender-identity-sexuality.html. https://perma.cc/Y8S9-6D7Q

competitions against women and girls. The federal government has announced that school showers, restrooms, locker rooms, and dormitories must be accessible based on self-professed "gender identity" rather than biological sex; if schools do not comply, they will be subjected to the full force of the United States Department of Justice. Even the American Medical Association — which continues to recognize the absolute necessity of making medical decisions based on biological sex — has advocated for the removal of biological sex as a legal designation on the public portion of birth certificates. (For clarity, this book uses the phrase "biological sex," but of course, there is no other type of sex.)

Second, gender ideology, ironically, enforces rigid stereotypes about what it means to be a male or female. For years, our society has encouraged girls to pursue activities that had once been stereotypically reserved for boys, like contact sports or careers in math, science, and politics. But gender activists would have a girl who likes to engage in formerly stereotypical male activities reconsider whether she is even a girl at all. If she develops a feeling or self-conception that she is a boy because of her interests, then activists say that she should consider being renamed, called by male pronouns, filled with testosterone, and undergo invasive surgery that permanently disfigures her body and leaves her infertile.

Third, it is wrong to think that gender ideology doesn't hurt anyone. Like any social movement that departs from God's plan for humanity, gender ideology leads to numerous, and significant, harms. It denies women and girls equal opportunity in athletics, scholarships, internships, and STEM-related programs. It deprives women — and men — of bodily privacy in intimate spaces and dormitories. It restricts free speech and threatens religious liberty. It breaks families apart, causing deep rifts between parents and children and spouses and other members of immediate and extended families. Parent-child rifts are further exacerbated by school officials who affirm students' professed gender identities without even informing parents what is happening during the school day.

Fourth, though it is rarely reported by the media or examined in popular entertainment, gender ideology also harms the individuals who suffer from clinical gender dysphoria — those who experience a sense of disharmony between their biological sex and societal gender expectations associated with that sex — the very people that gender ideology is supposed to benefit most. Puberty blockers stunt physical and brain development. Hormone injections may eventually result in permanent infertility. The best long-term study on the subject shows that suicide rates and psychiatric hospitalizations actually *increase* when individuals undergo a "gender transition."[4] And none of those facts should be surprising. After all, gender dysphoria is the only mental-health condition where society urges individuals to align their bodies with their minds rather than their minds with their bodies. We would never encourage a family member or friend afflicted with anorexia — an obsessive desire to lose weight often caused by the mistaken belief that one is overweight — to "be their true self" and eat less to lose weight.

Fifth, gender ideology matters because the whole foundation of faith and humanity is at stake. The basic relationship between men and women is not merely incidental to the structure of God's creation; it is a central feature, toward which all else is directed. The whole of creation and its purpose is summed up in its pinnacle — Adam and Eve and their nuptial relationship. To lose the centrality of this nuptial purpose of creation is to lose nature. And to lose nature is to lose the foundation of the sacraments, which is ultimately to lose the logic of the Church itself.

---

[4]   See Ryan T. Anderson, "Sex Reassignment Doesn't Work. Here Is the Evidence," *The Heritage Foundation*, March 9, 2018, https://www.heritage.org/gender/commentary/sex-reassignment-doesnt-work-here-the-evidence. https://perma.cc/8Y96-B69T

In sum, gender ideology causes innumerable harms and cannot simply be ignored. This is why the Catholic Church has spoken out so boldly against those who present a view of the human person that is so contrary to the truth. As Pope Francis has warned: "Today children — children! — are taught in school that everyone can choose his or her sex. Why are they teaching this?"[5] And again:

> Acceptance of our bodies ... is vital for welcoming and accepting the entire world as a gift ... whereas thinking that we enjoy absolute power over our own bodies turns, often subtly, into thinking that we enjoy absolute power over creation. Learning to accept our body, to care for it and to respect its fullest meaning, is an essential element of any genuine human ecology.[6]

What's more, Pope Francis continues, "valuing one's own body in its femininity or masculinity is necessary if I am going to be able to recognize myself in an encounter with someone who is different."[7] Yet that truth is precisely what gender ideology rejects, depriving us and anyone the Church seeks to evangelize of a natural or created understanding of reality.

The Catholic response: love

As disciples of Jesus Christ, it is important that we treat every person with love and dignity, recognizing that each one of us is made *imago Dei* — in the image and likeness of God. Yet it is equally important that we recognize what "love" really means. Love is not a feeling. Nor

---

5   Pope Francis, Address to the Polish Bishops (July 27, 2016); available at https://www.vatican.va/content/francesco/en/speeches/2016/july/documents/papa-francesco_20160727_polonia-vescovi.html. https://perma.cc/AG76-749P

6   Pope Francis, encyclical letter *Laudato Si'* (Care for Our Common Home) (May 24, 2015), no. 155.

7   Ibid.

is love merely giving someone everything he or she wants. Authentic Christian love is willing the good of the other. As every parent understands, it is never willing the good of the other to lie to them, to mislead them, or to give them what they ask when it will harm them. Rather, we must strive to be like Paul the Apostle and speak the truth in charity (see Eph. 4:15). And the truth about gender ideology is stark.

Bishop Michael Burbidge explains it well in the Diocese of Arlington's *A Catechesis on the Human Person and Gender Ideology*:

> The claim to "be transgender" or the desire to seek "transition" rests on a mistaken view of the human person, rejects the body as a gift from God, and leads to grave harm.... To affirm someone in an identity at odds with biological sex or to affirm a person's desired "transition" is to mislead that person. It involves speaking and interacting with that person in an untruthful manner.

And "in no circumstances," he concludes, "can we confirm a person in error," since doing so "does not resolve a person's struggles but also can in fact exacerbate them."[8]

The purpose of this book

The Church's teachings on this issue are true, good, and beautiful, because they show us how best to love others. But it can be hard to speak the truth and to love each other truly when the truth conflicts with the views of contemporary society. The Church's teachings also raise many reasonable questions. How can allowing someone to act in accord with their self-understanding or preference cause harm to

---

[8]   Bishop Michael F. Burbidge, *A Catechesis on the Human Person and Gender Ideology* (August 12, 2021); available at https://www.arlingtondiocese. org/Communications/Bishop/Public-Messages/A-Catechesis-on-the-Human-Person-and-Gender-Ideology-Catholic-Diocese-of-Arlington. pdf. https://perma.cc/Q2GS-RWKH

themselves and to others? Does the human body really have a purpose or nature that can be violated? If so, what is that purpose?

To answer these questions, we must remember that everything in the universe — every star, every tree, every *body* — proclaims some truth about its Maker. Just as finely created furniture or jewelry says something about its maker, every atom in the universe can help us discover the truth about God. And that includes the mysteries of the human body.

Pope St. John Paul II's Theology of the Body helps explain the truth that the human body reveals about God, and we will examine it closely. His theology provides a deep understanding of why the Church continues to teach the biblical principle that God made us "male and female" (Gen. 1:27).

We will also consider the meaning of freedom and of truth itself. In today's culture, many believe that freedom means being able to choose to do whatever they want, free from constraint or coercion. This understanding of freedom causes individuals to view morality as something restrictive, something that limits freedom. Worse, it places the individual at the center of meaning and disregards all responsibilities to God or to others. In the end, such "freedom" makes us slaves to our own selfishness, leads to loneliness, and makes us unhappy.

True freedom is freedom *for* something: namely, to choose to do what is good — which is to follow God's will. God has placed His truth in our hearts from the beginning, and through the Church, God has provided detailed instructions for how we should live as disciples of Christ. But these instructions can be ignored, and when we ignore them, the consequences are predictable: our lives, and our relationships with each other and with God, start to break and eventually stop working altogether. The result is the exact opposite of the joy and salvation that God wills for us.

This book is intended to help you navigate through the many questions surrounding gender ideology. We will begin by learning about what freedom really is and how the Church helps us to achieve it. Next, we will turn to what the Church teaches us about the human body and how the Church applies those teachings to gender ideology. That study will naturally evolve into the biology and philosophy regarding what it means to be male and female and what it means to "identify" as something other than your biological sex.

We will then begin to look at the personal, familial, and societal harms that gender ideology is causing. We will hear from those who eagerly embraced sex reassignment only to have deep regret and ultimately detransition, and then we will observe how the government, media, and societal forces have promoted this harmful ideology at the expense of the fundamental values our country has traditionally treasured. We will conclude with a comprehensive chapter that lists common questions about gender ideology and provides answers straight from American bishops and Church documents, including advice for those who have a family member, co-worker, or friend who is struggling with gender dysphoria.

With all that in mind, let us begin our journey with a discussion of authentic freedom and the importance of objective truth.

CHAPTER 1

What Is Truth?

♀ ♂

IN HIS THIRD AND last encyclical, *Caritas in Veritate* (Charity in Truth), Pope Benedict XVI explained that without truth, love becomes an "empty shell," and acts that we believe to be loving can in fact be cruel.[9] In other words, love without truth is not love at all.

Every parent intuitively understands this. Even if a child really, *really* wants to touch a hot stove burner, a loving parent would never allow their child to place a hand on the burner. Every parent knows a truth that the child does not yet understand: a hot stove will burn and hurt you. No amount of begging or insistence that "touching the stove will make me happy!" would possibly change the parent's mind.

But to love with truth requires that there is, in fact, an *objective* truth. In other words, it requires that certain things are true for all people, in all time, everywhere.

This understanding of truth is the exact opposite of what moral relativism claims. Moral relativism is the belief that there is

---

9   Pope Benedict XVI, encyclical letter *Caritas in Veritate* (June 29, 2009), no. 3.

no objective truth: what's true for you is true for you, and what's true for me is true for me. If someone believes that adultery is not wrong for them, then no one else can be critical if that person has an affair. Or if a 5' 9" American male professes that he is a 6' 5" Asian woman, then others cannot disagree with that belief, no matter how preposterous it seems.[10]

When asked what is "the greatest problem of our time," Pope Benedict did not cite war, abortion, euthanasia, lack of Mass attendance, spotty catechesis, or a disbelief of Jesus' Real Presence in the Eucharist. He answered, "moral relativism."[11] This chapter will contrast love and truth with moral relativism, explaining why moral relativism is incoherent, depressing, and harmful. It will then discuss how virtue, morality, and objective truth lead to true freedom.

What is love?

True love requires truth. But what is love? In many movies, television shows, and novels, love is most frequently portrayed as a dreamy, romantic feeling that makes you happy. Such love is rarely sacrificial, and it is almost always described in terms of an individual's emotions and their self-fulfillment rather than as a conscious, willed choice.

The *Catechism of the Catholic Church* explains love very differently: "To love is to will the good of another" (CCC 1766). This definition has several components. First, love is not a feeling but an intentional act. Love involves *choosing* to act in such a way that benefits another. Second, love always focuses on someone else. Love is not defined by how I benefit but by how someone else does. Third,

---

[10] Family Policy Institute of Washington, "Gender Identity: Can a 5'9, White Guy Be a 6'5, Chinese Woman?" YouTube Video, 4:13, April 13, 2016, https://www.youtube.com/watch?v=xfO1veFs6Ho. https://perma.cc/XB5H-VPYJ

[11] Chris Stefanick, *Absolute Relativism: The New Dictatorship and What to Do about It* (El Cajon, CA: Catholic Answers, 2011), 1.

love does not necessarily result in another's happiness but in their "good." In the case of the child and the hot stove, what the child *desires* is not the same as what will do them *good*. Sometimes another's good will coincide with that person's desire, but not always. Never confuse kindness with love.

Caritas in Veritate emphasizes that charity is "at the heart of the Church's social doctrine."[12] Pope Francis has echoed this sentiment, explaining that the Church must be like "a field hospital after battle. It is useless to ask a seriously injured person if he has high cholesterol and about the level of his blood sugar! You have to heal his wounds. Then we can talk about everything else."[13]

However, Pope Benedict's encyclical is called "Charity *in Truth*" because there is no charity without truth. Consider another example of charity: How should we help a close relative or friend who is an alcoholic? It would be not at all uncommon for an alcoholic to believe that he can only be happy and truly "himself" when intoxicated. But it would not be loving to encourage that close relative or friend to continue drinking or to drink even more excessively. He might be unable to keep a job, would likely alienate his family and close friends, and would probably die far too young because of illness or driving drunk. There is nothing loving or charitable about encouraging such outcomes; indeed, to do so would be cruel, just as Pope Benedict described.

What is the difference between truth and moral relativism?

Disturbingly, there are fewer and fewer people in America who believe there is an objective truth. In a 2016 survey, 57 percent of respondents said they believed that "whatever is right for your life or works best for you is the only truth you can know." Seventy-four percent of

---

[12] Pope Benedict XVI, *Caritas in Veritate*, no. 2.

[13] Pope Francis, "A Big Heart Open to God," *America Magazine*, September 30, 2013.

millennials affirmed that statement; shockingly, 31 percent of practicing Christians did so too. Likewise, 65 percent of U.S. adults affirmed that "every culture must determine what is acceptable morality for its people," and, not coincidentally, 69 percent agreed that "any kind of sexual expression between two consenting adults is acceptable."[14]

These beliefs are apparent if we look at how people talk about socially important or moral issues: "*For me,* abortion is wrong. But I would never tell someone else what they should do with their own body." "*For me,* adultery is wrong, but not everyone may agree." Is this not the same way we talk about our favorite dessert? "*For me,* chocolate chip is the best kind of cookie." Great moral truths such as the sacredness of life and fidelity in marriage are becoming mere opinions.

People like moral relativism because it appears to be nonjudgmental. It makes us feel that we are being inclusive of others; it seems to ensure that no one gets hurt by moral disagreements. But that is a big lie. Moral relativism does cause harm, because when we give up on objective moral truth, we distort our relationship with reality. Suddenly, anything seems morally justifiable. But this does not mean that we will be able to evade the natural consequences of our actions.

Moral relativism is also at its core a depressing and hopeless view of the world. If there is no good or evil, no right or wrong choice — if everything is merely good or bad "*for me*" — then our decisions do not ultimately matter. Relativism says that our lives have no real significance. *That* is a very discouraging philosophy by which to live your life.

14 Michael Foust, "One-Third of Practicing Christians Say Morality Is Relative, Shocking Poll Shows," *Christian Examiner,* May 31, 2016, https://www.christianexaminer.com/news/one-third-of-practicing-christians-say-morality-is-relative-shocking-poll-shows.html. https://perma.cc/Y256-TTLW

We were made to ask the big questions: For what purpose do I exist? What happens to me when I die? Is there an all-powerful God who loves me?[15] If we accept the lie that life has no meaning, that this is all there is, we're led into what Pope St. John Paul II described as "a sad loneliness in which [we] are deprived of reasons for hope and are incapable of real love."[16]

Relativism *seems* to let us off the hook when we fail to do what we know to be right and true, but this is deceptive. We're still on the hook, because our actions still really do have consequences, even if we pretend that what is immoral is moral. Drug use, abortion, cheating on your taxes — some think we do not need to feel guilty for engaging in these objectively bad behaviors because they are not wrong "for me." But like any deal with the devil, that dispensation comes at a profound cost: the loss of meaning and purpose to your life, perhaps even the loss of your soul.

Indeed, moral relativism undermines the very right to life, and not just life in utero. As Pope St. John Paul II recognized, the right to life itself becomes a matter of popular will — a mere vote — as "the sinister result of a relativism which reigns unopposed: the 'right' ceases to be such, because it is no longer firmly founded on the inviolable dignity of the person."[17] When the right to life is a matter of personal opinion, it is possible for a society to take innocent life before it is born. Or when it becomes old or infirm. Or when it is disabled. Or if it is the wrong sex, race, or economic class. Or when a life is simply inconvenient.

Finally, moral relativism eliminates God from our lives altogether. If we believe that God is objectively all powerful, all knowing,

---

[15] See Chris Stefanick and Paul McCusker, *The Search* (Greenwood Village, CO: Augustine Institute, 2020).

[16] Stefanick, *Absolute Relativism*, 8.

[17] Pope St. John Paul II, encyclical letter *Evangelium Vitae* (March 25, 1995), no. 20.

all good, and all loving, we cannot believe that His nature depends on what we think about Him, or even what most people think about Him. And how can we believe that God made us "to know Him, to love Him, and to serve Him in this world, and to be happy with Him forever in Heaven" — as we should[18] — if God is simply a product of group belief rather than Someone who actually *is*?

In sum, moral relativism is a dead-end philosophy that is not worthy of our lives and is not worth following. But if not moral relativism, then what moral system should we believe?

Classical moral worldview

The best alternative to moral relativism is the classical moral worldview.[19] Philosophers and religious scholars have contemplated the truth of this worldview for more than two thousand years, starting with Plato and Aristotle, then reaching new heights with St. Thomas Aquinas, the beloved Dominican friar who wrote *Summa Theologica*. In essence, the classical moral worldview considers the world to be ordered, good, and intelligible. It teaches that there are objective moral truths that humans can discern and understand in any age, time, or place. And the classical moral worldview instructs that we can only achieve true happiness by following these truths, which draw us closer to God and allow us to become the best possible versions of ourselves.[20]

To understand objective moral truth and put it into action, we must start with the idea of *telos* (pronounced "teh-loss"), a Greek word that means the "purpose" or "end" of something. Our lives have a purpose that God engraved on the heart of every one of us:

[18] "Lesson First: On the End of Man, Question and Answer 6," *Baltimore Catechism No. 1* (Catholic Book Publishing, 1964).

[19] See Edward Sri, *Who Am I to Judge?: Responding to Relativism with Logic and Love* (San Francisco: Ignatius Press, 2016).

[20] For more detail on the classical moral worldview, see appendix one.

we were made to be in relationship — with God and each other. But we are not disembodied spirits; we are embodied souls. So God made our *bodies* for a reason. They have a purpose too — and it is explained by the Theology of the Body, Pope St. John Paul II's great teaching about the Christian vocation to love.[21] That is the topic to which we turn next.

---

[21] A free, online edition of Pope St. John Paul II's teachings on the Theology of the Body can be found at https://stmarys-waco.org/documents/2016/9/theology_of_the_body.pdf (The Catholic Primer, 2006). https://perma.cc/AL88-LBEH

CHAPTER 2

How the Human Body Helps Us Understand God's Nature

"THEOLOGY" SIMPLY MEANS "THE study of God." So "Theology of the Body" is the study of God as revealed through the human body. This theology comes from a series of 129 weekly addresses that Pope St. John Paul II gave to papal audiences in Rome from September 5, 1979, through November 28, 1984. These addresses stand in stark contrast to the American sexual revolution of the 1960s.

The thesis of the Theology of the Body is as simple as it is startling. Each of us is a unity of body and soul. And "the body, in fact, and only the body," says Pope St. John Paul II, "is capable of making visible what is invisible: the spiritual and divine. It has been created to transfer into the visible reality of the world the mystery hidden from eternity in God, and thus to be a sign of it."[22] As Christopher

---

22 Pope St. John Paul II, *Man and Woman He Created Them: A Theology of the Body*, trans. Michael Waldstein (Boston: Pauline Books and Media, 2006), 19.4.

West puts it, "somehow the body enables us to 'see' spiritual realities, even the eternal mystery 'hidden' in God."[23] That's quite a claim!

The *Catechism* explains that "God himself is an eternal exchange of love, Father, Son, and Holy Spirit, and he has destined us to share in that exchange" (CCC 221). At the foundation of the Theology of the Body is the notion that the love between a married man and woman is called to be a "created version" of the Trinity's own "eternal exchange of love." That is why the Bible uses spousal love more than any other image to help us understand God's relationship to humanity.[24]

God wanted this plan to be so obvious to us that He actually impressed an image of it in our very being by creating us male and female and calling us to communion "in one flesh." In Genesis 1:28, when God directs us to be "fruitful and multiply," our cultural mandate, He is calling us to live in His own image, to love as He loves.[25] This chapter will explore the Theology of the Body in detail and will introduce concepts that will be further developed in the following chapter, which addresses more specific teachings about gender ideology.

The beginning

In Genesis 1, God created light and darkness, Heaven and earth, plants and fish, birds and animals. And as He did so, God looked at what He was creating and "saw that it was good" (Gen. 1:4, 10, 18, 21, 25). Indeed, surveying man and the entirety of creation, God observed that "it was *very* good" (Gen. 1:31; emphasis added).

---

[23] Christopher West, *Theology of the Body for Beginners: A Basic Introduction to Pope John Paul II's Sexual Revolution, Revised Edition* (West Chester, PA: Ascension Press, 2009), 6.

[24] E.g., Hosea 2:19: "And I will betroth you to me forever. I will betroth you to me in righteousness and in justice, in steadfast love and in mercy."

[25] "By their very nature, the institute of matrimony itself and conjugal love are ordained for the procreation and education of children." Vatican Council II, Pastoral Constitution on the Church in the Modern World *Gaudium et Spes* (December 7, 1965), no. 48.

But in Genesis 2, when the Bible gives us a closer, more detailed look at God's creation of man, something changes. After God created Adam, placed him in the Garden of Eden, and instructed him not to eat of the tree of the knowledge of good and evil, God saw that "it is *not* good" (Gen. 2:18; emphasis added). What's not good? "That the man should be alone" (Gen. 2:18). This is the first time that God saw a problem in what He had created.

At first glance, this observation seems confusing. After all, man was surrounded by other creatures that God had created. With many companions on the land, in the sea, and in the air, Adam was hardly in existence by himself. So why did God conclude that Adam was alone? Because Adam was the only bodily creature made in God's image and likeness. As a human, he was distinctly different than a fish, a bird, a lion, or a chimpanzee. So God decided to make a suitable "helper" for the man (Gen. 2:18).

In English, a "helper" sounds like an assistant or servant — someone who is subservient. But the word in Hebrew is *ezer* (pronounced "ay-zer"). And that word is always used in the Old Testament to describe someone who provides vitally important and powerful acts of rescue and support. In fact, the Old Testament uses the word *ezer* sixteen times in reference to *God Himself* as a helper! This "helper" is not just an assistant but someone who will be vital to support and rescue the man from his condition of being alone. It will allow Adam both to pursue and to realize the two-fold vocation that Jesus Christ describes in Mark 12:29–31: to love God and to love his neighbor.

Search for a helper

That begs another question. Why did the man need rescuing? True, he was alone; but is that intrinsically bad? The answer is yes! As God was preparing to create man, He said, "Let us make man in *our* image, after *our* likeness" (Gen. 1:26; emphasis added). That's because God is an eternal exchange of love between the Father, the Son, and the

Holy Spirit. Since man shares that image and likeness, he too is created and called to be in relationship — one of selfless love, willing only the good of another. So when God declared it is "not good" for man to be alone, He meant it. Without the kind of relationship that God intended, man cannot fulfill the purpose for which God created him.

Adam needed another human being to enter this relationship. After Adam expressed dominion over all the creatures of the land, sea, and air by giving the creatures their names, Genesis informs us that "there was not found a helper fit for him" (Gen. 2:20). So God put Adam into a deep sleep, took one of his ribs, and used that rib to make a woman.

Upon seeing her, Adam exclaimed immediately: "This at last is bone of my bones and flesh of my flesh; she shall be called Woman, because she was taken out of Man" (Gen. 2:23). Note that the man is immediately drawn to the woman's *body* and their shared humanity. Both are persons made in God's image and likeness. Both are "alone" in the created world because they are different from all the other creatures. And both are called to live in an eternal covenant of love.

But there's more. You see, the man and the woman were *not* identical. When God created man in His image, "male and female he created them" (Gen. 1:27). And in their nakedness, it was immediately obvious to each of them that they were complementary. As Emily Stimpson Chapman beautifully wrote, "In that [unclothed] state, man not only could read the metaphor of the body rightly, but also read it without thought, easily and naturally, almost like breathing."[26]

Think about that for a moment. As others have noted, every one of us has a circulatory system, a respiratory system, a muscular system, and so on, and each system works perfectly fine all on its own; but no human being, alone, has a reproductive system — only *one-half* a

[26] Emily Stimpson, *These Beautiful Bones: An Everyday Theology of the Body* (Steubenville, OH: Emmaus Road Publishing, 2013), 34.

system. In other words, our reproductive organs can only perform their biological function when a man and a woman come together in a conjugal relationship. And in their nakedness, Adam and Eve could immediately perceive God's plan for their togetherness *through their bodies* — a plan that is plainly apparent even to the most skeptical atheist.

God's first commission to mankind

After creating Adam and Eve male and female, God's very first instruction to them — indeed, His first commandment — was "be fruitful and multiply and fill the earth and subdue it" (Gen. 1:28). This is our cultural mandate. And this is why "a man shall leave his father and his mother and hold fast to his wife, and they shall become one flesh" (Gen. 2:24); that is, they will have a conjugal relationship. That beautiful observation in Genesis is echoed by Jesus in Matthew 19:5 and Mark 10:7–8 and also by St. Paul in Ephesians 5:31. (Do not let anyone try to persuade you that the New Testament does not address the meaning of marriage.)

When a man and a woman become "one body" in a sacramental marriage, they can be a selfless gift to each other emotionally, spiritually, and physically. They hold nothing back, even their reproductive capacity — which is why the Church has consistently taught that contraception is wrong.[27] In fact, the Church has expressed this teaching as an infallible doctrine:

> The Church has always taught the intrinsic evil of contraception, that is, of every marital act intentionally rendered

---

[27] See Pope St. Paul VI, encyclical letter *Humanae Vitae* (Human Life) (July 25, 1968), no. 14: "We are obliged once more to declare that the direct interruption of the generative process already begun and, above all, all direct abortion, even for therapeutic reasons, are to be absolutely excluded as lawful means of regulating the number of children. Equally to be condemned, as the magisterium of the Church has affirmed on many occasions, is direct sterilization, whether of the man or of the woman, whether permanent or temporary"; cf. CCC 2370, 2399.

unfruitful. This teaching is to be held as definitive and ir-
reformable. Contraception is gravely opposed to marital
chastity, it is contrary to the good of the transmission of
life (the procreative aspect of matrimony), and to the re-
ciprocal self-giving of the spouses (the unitive aspect of
matrimony); it harms true love and denies the sovereign
role of God in the transmission of human life.[28]

To state it in the affirmative, the conjoining of a man and woman in
a sacramental marriage allows them to participate in God's creation
by co-creating with Him to make a new life, and we should not thwart
the magnificence of that design.

It is now possible to glimpse some of the beauty of being made
in the image and likeness of God. From the eternal exchange of love
between God the Father and God the Son proceeds God the Holy
Spirit, each of Them a distinct Person yet still one God. Similarly, as
many have observed, the love between a man and woman in a sacramental marriage can be so strong that it will require its own name: a
"son" or "daughter." Turning to Christopher West, even though God
is not a sexual being, human "marital union [i.e., the communion of
persons established by marriage] is meant to be an icon in some way
of the inner life of the Trinity!"[29]

And that is not the only imaging taking place. Recall that in
Genesis 1:26, God said, "Let us make man in our image, after our
likeness." Several chapters later, in Genesis 5:3, Adam became a
first-time father, and this is how the Bible describes it: "When
Adam had lived 130 years, he fathered a son in his own likeness,
after his image." By drawing a parallel between Adam's paternity
and God's paternity, the Bible emphasizes that:

[28] Pontifical Council for the Family, *Vademecum for Confessors Concerning
Some Aspects of the Morality of Conjugal Life* (February 12, 1997), 2.4.
[29] Christopher West, *Theology of the Body for Beginners*, 25.

man's fatherhood generates in a way that parallels the
generativity of God. When God made Adam and Eve and
inscribed into their being the call to be fruitful, then, he
was inscribing a part of himself into humanity. Human
generation is not simply a mechanism for procreation; it
is sharing in the very life of God.[30]

Yet there is still more. When a child is born, "both of the spouses receive
[not only] an image of themselves, but they also receive, again, and in
a new way, their spouse," explains author Melinda Selmys.[31] That is
why, in times of adversity and stress, children help keep a married couple
together. Spouses are "able to find the man or woman they once loved
in the faces, gestures, works, and personality of their child. The child
is a constant rediscovery of the mystery of spousal love, and each child
that is born expresses this in a different way."[32]

One final note before we leave our tour through Genesis. Although Adam and Eve were both naked in the Garden of Eden, Genesis 2:25 makes clear that they "were not ashamed." Why? Because
shame is a natural self-defense against being treated as an object of
sexual use. Before Original Sin, lust — that is, *self*-seeking sexual desire, the exact opposite of selfless love — had not yet entered the
human heart.

That all changed with the Fall. Now Adam and Eve immediately
felt ashamed. They were threatened by their nakedness because it
made them vulnerable to lust, even from each other. So they felt
compelled to immediately cover themselves. Adam and Eve no longer saw themselves exclusively as a gift to the other because lust
"tramples on the ruins" of the body's spousal meaning and instead

---

[30] Fr. Carter Griffin, *Why Celibacy? Reclaiming the Fatherhood of the Priest*
(Steubenville, OH: Emmaus Road Publishing, 2019), 14.
[31] Melinda Selmys, *Sexual Authenticity: An Intimate Reflection on Homosexuality and Catholicism* (Huntington, IN: Our Sunday Visitor, 2009), 136.
[32] Ibid., 136–37.

seeks only to satisfy the body's "sexual urge."[33] In contrast, when Adam and Eve *first* saw each other naked, neither was a threat to the other's innocence and dignity. They were "free with the very freedom of the gift," as Pope St. John Paul II explained it.[34]

In sum, before Original Sin, Adam and Eve saw only God's plan of selfless love. This plan was inscribed in their naked bodies and gave them the ability to give themselves freely, sincerely, and totally as a gift to the other — to image or be an icon of the eternal exchange of love between the Father, the Son, and the Holy Spirit. This is the spousal meaning of the human body: the love of a man and woman — and *only* a man and woman — is fruitful. Life-giving. In that way, it is God-like. Divine. It is why marriage must, and can, be only between one man and one woman.

The purpose of our bodies

Once we see the divine origin and destiny of our bodies, how we should think about and use our human bodies becomes clear. When we use our bodies as God has ordained, we are fulfilling the purpose for which God created us. We can be the best possible version of ourselves, and we can be co-creators with God of life itself. The self-giving love of the Trinity — Father, Son, and Holy Spirit — becomes the model for familial love.

The modern sexual movement rejects such a view of the body. Unsurprisingly, that has resulted in a false freedom, one that diminishes marriage, children, and families. As Emily Stimpson Chapman explains it, modernism sees children as merely the biological result of having sex, products to be enjoyed or aborted rather than recognized and honored as sacred gifts. Such a view reflects selfish pursuit of whatever feels good, no matter the cost to others. Indeed

---

[33] Pope St. John Paul II, *Man and Woman He Created Them*, 40.4.
[34] Ibid., 15.1.

that same selfishness "is why the suffering of ailing and aging parents, of poverty, disease, broken marriages, and wounded hearts has become, for multitudes of men, meaningless pain, to be avoided at all costs, never accepted, never embraced, never offered up for our own and others' salvation."[35]

Remarkably, someone accurately predicted — decades ahead of time — that ignoring God's plan for the body and human sexuality would end in great social disaster. In one of the most prophetic reflections of the entire twentieth century, Pope St. Paul VI, in his *Humanae Vitae*, discerned through natural law, logic, and the Holy Spirt what was likely to happen to our society if the Church abandoned its rule prohibiting contraception and allowed the culture to sever the procreation and rearing of children from the sexual union of husband and wife. As you read these predictions, consider the state of modern society and recall that Pope St. Paul VI wrote these words in 1968:

> Responsible men can become more deeply convinced of the truth of the doctrine laid down by the Church on this issue if they reflect on the consequences of methods and plans for artificial birth control. Let them first consider how easily this course of action could open wide the way for *marital infidelity* and *a general lowering of moral standards*. Not much experience is needed to be fully aware of human weakness and to understand that human beings — and especially the young, who are so exposed to temptation — need incentives to keep the moral law, and it is an evil thing to make it easy for them to break that law. Another effect that gives cause for alarm is that a man who grows accustomed to the use of contraceptive methods may *forget the reverence due to a woman*, and, disregarding her physical and emotional equilibrium, *reduce her to being a mere instrument for the satisfaction of his own*

---

[35] Emily Stimpson, *These Beautiful Bones*, 19.

desires, no longer considering her as his partner whom he should surround with care and affection.

Finally, careful consideration should be given to the danger of this power passing into the hands of those public authorities who care little for the precepts of the moral law. Who will blame a government which in its attempt to resolve the problems affecting an entire country resorts to the same measures as are regarded as lawful by married people in the solution of a particular family difficulty? *Who will prevent public authorities from favoring those contraceptive methods which they consider more effective?* Should they regard this as necessary, *they may even impose their use on everyone.* It could well happen, therefore, that when people, either individually or in family or social life, experience the inherent difficulties of the divine law and are determined to avoid them, *they may give into the hands of public authorities the power to intervene in the most personal and intimate responsibility of husband and wife.*[36]

From the #MeToo movement to society's dramatically falling marriage rates, from broken families to the U.S. federal government's intrusive attempts to force every employer in the country (even nunneries) to provide contraception and abortion coverage in employee health plans, Pope St. Paul VI's predictions have come true in the wake of the widespread acceptance in the 1960s and 1970s of the idea that sex and procreation were independent concepts.

But in a way, it is understandable. American culture tries to ingrain in us the mistaken idea that freedom is the ability to do whatever we want. But this is not true freedom. As the *Catechism* instructs, "freedom is the power, rooted in reason and will, to act or not to act, to do this or that, and so to perform deliberate actions on one's own responsibility.... There is no true freedom except in the service of

---

[36] Pope St. Paul VI, *Humanae Vitae*, no. 17; emphasis added.

what is good and just. The choice to disobey and do evil is an abuse of freedom and leads to 'the slavery of sin' " (*CCC* 1731, 1733). Or, as Lord Acton put it, "liberty is not the power of doing what we like, but the right of being able to do what we ought."

Think about it this way. LeBron James is one of the greatest basketball players who has ever played the game. But what makes him great is not the freedom to do whatever he wants. LeBron cannot cross a sideline or end line without having to give the ball to the other team. The same is true if he chooses to dribble, stop, and then dribble again. He cannot score points by passing the ball to a spectator. His freedom is "limited" by countless rules of professional basketball.

But those very same rules are what give LeBron the ability to be a great player. Otherwise, there would be no way to tell that he has scored and assisted on more baskets and rebounded more basketballs than almost anyone who has ever played in the NBA. And even if he had great dribbling and shooting skills, if there were no rules, someone bigger and stronger than LeBron could simply tackle him before he took a single shot. Perhaps surprisingly, the Bible addresses this important point explicitly in Paul's Second Letter to Timothy: "An athlete is not crowned unless he competes according to the rules" (2 Tim. 2:5).

Many people outside the Church — and perhaps some of those in the Church — assume that God's rules about marriage, sexuality, and protecting human life are simply arbitrary decrees that we have to follow, or that God's laws are some test of obedience that will result in punishment if we break them. That could not be further from the truth. God's moral law is really about *love*. God made the moral law — and the virtues necessary to follow it — because He loves us and wants us to have *true* freedom.

The moral law is a bit like an owner's manual for a car. An owner's manual is a lengthy list of rules — like a "catechism" — written by the people who designed the car, those who know best what actions we need to take (and not take) for it to work well.

We do not *have* to follow the manual's rules; we can just leave those directives in the glove box. But if we neglect the rules, the car will break down, and, at some point, it will stop working altogether. Yet no one views a car's owner's manual as an imposition created to restrict freedom or as a test of obedience that will result in punishment by the car's creator if ignored. To the contrary, the rules are made to help maximize the car's usefulness and value.

In the same way, God's moral law is the way to achieve our *telos*: our end purpose and true happiness. In a morally relativistic culture, many people doubt that God's law is really a trustworthy pathway to happiness in life. Like Adam and Eve, we all think we know a better way. But when we reject God's moral law and replace it with our own ideas and personal preferences, we reject God's loving care for us, and things predictably start to break down. Just look around at our culture. That is why Pope St. John Paul II instructed: "Do not accept anything as the truth if it lacks love. And do not accept anything as love which lacks truth! One without the other becomes a destructive lie."[37]

Pope Francis says the same thing a little differently: "relativism wounds people."[38] And Christians are called to go out into the world armed with charity and truth to heal those wounds and proclaim the wonderful alternative that God provides. That calling includes Church teachings about how to treat others, how to conduct ourselves, God's plan for marriage, the importance of family, and countless other things.

---

[37] Pope St. John Paul II, *Homily for the Canonization of Edith Stein* (October 11, 1998).

[38] Pope Francis, *The Name of God is Mercy*, trans. Oonagh Stransky (New York: Random House, 2016), 15.

Celibacy and infertility

It is important to emphasize that marriage and procreation are not the only ways that we can "image" God's love. As Christopher West explains, "they serve as the original model, but whenever we imitate Christ in 'giving up our bodies' for others, we express the spousal meaning."[39] For example, a priest's vow of celibacy "is not a rejection of sexuality. It is a call to embrace the meaning and purpose of sexuality": "the eternal union of Christ and the Church."[40] To paraphrase the teachings of Pope St. John Paul II, "priests and consecrated religious who take a vow of celibacy *affirm* marriage's goodness because it is such a great sacrifice to give up something as wonderful as the marriage sacrament."[41]

And that, of course, is the goal for all of us. The sacrament of Marriage and conjugal union direct us to what Revelation 19:7 calls the "marriage of the Lamb." God created the sexes and their union to foreshadow what it will be like for us to live in Heaven. And "only the eternal, ecstatic, 'marriage' of Heaven — so far superior to anything proper to earthly life that we cannot begin to fathom it — can satisfy the human 'ache' of solitude."[42]

But this forces us to ask why a transgender individual could not simply image God's love in an appropriately complementary union. To answer that question, let us turn to the Church's teaching about gender ideology.

---

[39] Christopher West, *Theology of the Body for Beginners*, 29.

[40] Ibid. (referencing Ephesians 5:31–32).

[41] Pope St. John Paul II, *Man and Woman He Created Them*, 78–81; emphasis added.

[42] Christopher West, *Theology of the Body for Beginners*, 55.

CHAPTER 3

The Church and Gender Ideology

THE FOUNDATIONAL IDEA OF the Theology of the Body is that we are not merely disembodied souls that take up residence in a meaningless vessel that happens to be the human body. That is, we are not souls trapped in shells. Rather, we are embodied souls, and who we are is inextricably linked to our bodies: "The structure of [man's] body permits him to be the author of a truly human activity. In this activity *the body expresses the person*."[43] Everyone understands this body-soul unity intuitively. If someone slaps you in the face, you do not yell, "You hurt the body that I'm residing in!" Instead, you cry, "You hurt *me*!" Indeed, the body is so integral "to who we are as human beings that the body and soul *together* are fashioned and 'destined to live forever,'" as we affirm every week at Mass in the Nicene Creed.[44]

---

[43] Pope St. John Paul II, *Man and Woman He Created Them*, 7.2.

[44] Archbishop Jerome Edward Listecki, *Catechesis and Policy on Questions Concerning Gender Theory* (January 20, 2022), 2.1, available at https://www.archmil.org/ArchMil/attachments/2022GenderTheoryfinal.pdf
https://perma.cc/7P7T-CZ44

Espousing the belief that individuals can "feel" a gender different than what their bodies "are" is a modern expression of a very old, second-century heresy: Gnosticism. Gnostics believed that the body and soul were independent of each other, so the entire point of the spiritual life was to acquire the knowledge, or *gnosis*, to facilitate the escape of the soul from the body. In fact, one of the primary tenets of Gnosticism was that matter — including the body — is evil or bad.

In stark contrast, Biblical Christianity teaches that all matter is good because God created it. This includes the body. Indeed, after Jesus' Resurrection, He appeared to the apostles and *proved* He was still embodied: He showed them where the spear had entered His side and where the nails had punctured His feet and hands. He even asked for food and ate it in front of them to show them that He was not a ghost — that is, not a disembodied soul — but His embodied self.

And so the Church has always taught that our bodies are important. In fact, they are so important that at the end of time, *our own* bodies will be resurrected in Heaven. In other words, our bodies are not only not bad, they are sacred; we are a unity of our body and soul. If the material world were merely something to be "escaped," as Gnostics believed, then it would make no sense that God would feed us with Jesus' Body and Blood, under the species of bread and wine, to sustain us on our journey.[45]

---

[45] The Catholic Faith considers the Eucharist to be the "source and summit of the Christian life" because "in the blessed Eucharist is contained the whole spiritual good of the Church, namely Christ himself" (CCC 1324). And because we are material beings, matter matters (so to speak). The bread and wine that become Jesus' Body and Blood are prefigured by the king-priest Melchizedek in the Old Testament (CCC 1333). Moreover, "in the Old Covenant bread and wine were offered in sacrifice among the first fruits of the earth as a sign of grateful acknowledgment to the Creator." Finally, the bread is representative of the manna, the "daily bread" that represented "the fruit of the promised land" for the nation of Israel in the desert, and the wine is representative of the " 'cup of blessing' at the end of the Jewish Passover meal" signifying "the messianic expectation of the rebuilding of Jerusalem." In sum, "when Jesus instituted the Eucharist, he gave a new and definitive meaning to the blessing of the bread and the cup" (CCC 1334).

If "the body expresses the person," then our sex matters, and more than in just a biological way: different bodies mean different persons. This does not mean that either sex is superior to the other; both men and women have equal dignity because they image God. But as Emily Stimpson Chapman explains, men and women love, reason, and create in different ways. But those differences "aren't intended to divide us; they're intended to unite us. They're complementary. The way we love, reason, and create, the way we live in the world as women or men, is *enriched* by the way the other sex does the same. It's made complete, whole, and perfect in company with the other."[46]

The beauty and complementarity of male and female bodies provides the foundation for what the Church teaches us about gender ideology. Because "our bodies have been entrusted to us as gifts so we might more fully image God's unity," the Church teaches "that any therapies which would attempt to change the body into the opposite sex are forms of mutilation and are morally prohibited."[47]

What is meant by "gender identity"?

Before we jump into the details of the Church's teaching, it is important to pause and define the terms we will be discussing. Specifically, we need to understand the difference between "sex," which is a straightforward term, and "gender identity," which decidedly is not.[48] We'll be digging deeper into what scientific study has to say about these terms in the next chapter and so will keep the discussion here at a high level of generality.

---

[46] Emily Stimpson, *These Beautiful Bones*, 30; emphasis added.

[47] Diocese of Lansing, *Theological Guide: The Human Person and Gender Dysphoria* (January 15, 2021), 16; available at https://www.flipsnack. com/dolmi/theological-guide-the-human-person-and-gender-dysphoria. html. https://perma.cc/M32K-QQLY

[48] The following information is adapted from "FAQs," *Person and Identity: A Project of the Ethics and Public Policy Center*, https://personandidentity. com/the-basics/. https://perma.cc/U6AC-6E39

"Sex" is a biological classification of male or female, identified by a person's reproductive role and determined by chromosomes. At conception, a human egg — which always carries an X chromosome — is fertilized by a sperm that can carry either an X or a Y chromosome. An XY chromosomal combination means the baby is male. An XX chromosomal combination means the baby is female. When all goes well, these chromosome combinations tell the body how to develop so that the baby has a male or female reproductive system and a male or female body.

When a baby is born, its sex is not subjectively "assigned" but objectively acknowledged by the doctor. And while there are rare disorders of sexual development — a subject we'll address in a later chapter — that does not change the binary nature of sex as male and female. Beginning at conception, "every cell [of the person's body] has a sex," and that sex, whether male or female, cannot be changed by anyone.[49]

In the 1950s, psychologist John Money pioneered and began promoting a theory that each person also has a "gender identity" that is distinct from their sex. Today, the American Psychological Association defines the concept as "an internal sense of being male, female, or something else, which may or may not correspond to an individual's sex assigned at birth or sex characteristics."[50] Because "gender identity" is an internal sense, it is not objectively verifiable, as is sex, but (according to gender activists) it can be subjectively declared. So whereas "sex"

[49]   Institute of Medicine (U.S.) Committee on Understanding the Biology of Sex and Gender Differences, "Every Cell Has a Sex," in *Exploring the Biological Contributions to Human Health: Does Sex Matter?*, eds. Theresa M. Wizemann and Mary-Lou Pardue (Washington, DC: National Academies Press, 2001). 2, Every Cell Has a Sex. See https://www.ncbi.nlm.nih.gov/books/NBK222291/. https://perma.cc/G68H-VXRG

[50]   American Psychological Association, "A Glossary: Defining Transgender Terms," *Monitor on Psychology* 49, no. 8 (September 2018): 32; see https://www.apa.org/monitor/2018/09/ce-corner-glossary. https://perma.cc/Z6PD-3YLR

is our given nature and readily recognized in nearly all cases, "gender identity" is a vague and fluid concept based on our ability or inability to identify with certain social stereotypes.

Gender-identity proponents say that any of the dozens of possible gender identities are normal, healthy, and worthy of respect. This includes genders such as "androgyne" (an identity that is either both feminine and masculine or between the two), "genderqueer" (an identity that does not match societal expectations for the person's sex), "omnigender" (someone who possesses and experiences all genders), and "Two Spirit" (an identity that encompasses different genders and sexualities in Indigenous Native American cultures).[51] To these proponents, a person who identifies with their biological sex is "cisgender."[52]

If gender-identity proponents were simply saying that individuals have personalities that reflect different aspects of traditional gender norms to varying degrees, we might be able to write the entire debate off as a semantic exercise. The problem is, gender-identity advocates want the external physical world — from physical bodies to shared public spaces — to reflect the internal mental beliefs of those who say they are transgender.

Given the unintuitive nature of gender-identity proponents' claims about identity and the human body, it will likely be unsurprising to learn that the genesis of the entire movement is unethical research that does not even support John Money's claim that "gender identity" exists independently of sexual identity. Money's main study on gender identity involved identical twins, one of whom suffered irreparable damage to his reproductive organs from a circumcision as an infant and was "transitioned" and raised as a girl without being told about the procedure or his

---

[51] Veronica Zambon, "What Are Some Different Types of Gender Identity?" *MedicalNewsToday*, November 5, 2020, medicalnewstoday.com/articles/types-of-gender-identity. https://perma.cc/D8MN-2XQR

[52] Ibid.

true identity. The transitioned twin claimed that Money forced the twin boys to reenact sexual positions and photographed them doing so "to reinforce Money's theories on gender fluidity."[53] Sadly, the transitioned twin suffered severe psychological trauma and ultimately committed suicide. Anticipating today's gender activists, Money dismissed the twin's complaints "as antifeminist and anti-trans bias."[54]

The problem with Money's belief in a self-determined "gender identity" is that it creates a conflict between identity and body. As noted, this is akin to modern-day Gnosticism: our soul (or even, as secularists might describe it, our internal sense of self) is the "real me." While our bodies might be aligned or in conflict with that real me, say these Gnostics, our bodies are ultimately irrelevant to who we are.

But unlike changing the color of our hair, or getting a tattoo, or replacing a kidney, our body's sexed nature gives us a distinctly male or female identity; no amount of body manipulation can change that. To believe in a "gender identity" that is distinct from our sex, and which requires body modification to accommodate it, is necessarily to believe that God's creation of our body is intrinsically flawed or mistaken, and we therefore have to take it on ourselves to fix that mistake. Accordingly, gender ideology is fundamentally at odds with the Church's teaching that the body expresses the person and that "everyone, man and woman, should acknowledge and accept his sexual *identity*" (CCC 2333).[55]

---

53 Phil Gaetano, "David Reimer and John Money Gender Reassignment Controversy: The John/Joan Case," *The Embryo Project Encyclopedia*, November 15, 2017, embryo.asu.edu/pages/David-reimer-and-john-money-gender-reassignment-controversy-johnjoan-case. https://perma.cc/5LXQ-ZJVC

54 Ibid.

55 To reject gender ideology is *not* to reject the reality of gender dysphoria, which, though affecting a tiny percentage of human beings, is a real affliction in which someone wrongly perceives themselves to have been born in the wrong body.

The problems with separating sex and gender

As mentioned at the outset of this book, the Congregation for Catholic Education in 2019 published *Male and Female He Created Them: Towards a Path of Dialogue on the Question of Gender Theory in Education.* The document begins by acknowledging that in modern culture, "*sex* and *gender* are no longer synonyms or interchangeable concepts, since they are used to describe two different realities. Sex is seen as defining which of the two biological categories (deriving from the original feminine-masculine [pair]) one belonged to. Gender, on the other hand, would be the way in which the differences between the sexes are lived in culture."[56]

"The problem," the document continues, "does not lie in the distinction between the two terms, which can be interpreted correctly, but in *the separation of sex from gender*."[57] In other words, they become words that describe two distinct categories that can be mixed and matched at will. The result "is that the individual should be able to choose his or her own status, and that society should limit itself to guaranteeing this right, and even providing material support, since the minorities involved would otherwise suffer negative social discrimination."[58]

The Congregation acknowledges that the Church and gender-ideology proponents "share a laudable desire to combat all expressions of unjust discrimination."[59] But as we've discussed at length, to truly act in love always requires abiding in truth; loving always means living in reality (created and extolled as "good" by God) and helping others to do so. And the truth is that the "underlying presuppositions of [gender-ideology] theories can be traced back to a

---

[56] Congregation for Catholic Education, *Male and Female He Created Them*, no. 11.

[57] Ibid.

[58] Ibid., no. 14.

[59] Ibid., no. 15.

dualistic anthropology, separating body (reduced to the status of inert matter) from human will, which itself becomes an absolute that can manipulate the body as it pleases."[60] And this "combination of physicalism and voluntarism gives rise to relativism, in which everything that exists is of equal value and at the same time undifferentiated, without any real order or purpose."[61]

We already know where such relativism leads: "These ideas are the expression of a widespread way of thinking and acting in today's culture that confuses 'genuine freedom with the idea that each individual can act arbitrarily as if there were no truths, values, and principles to provide guidance, and everything were possible and permissible.'"[62] And in some cases, it can also lead to stereotypical rigidity: a girl who climbs trees and likes sports *must be* a boy, and a boy who likes to "play house" *must be* a girl.

In contrast, explains the Church, "the Holy Scripture reveals the wisdom of the Creator's design," which assigns "masculinity and femininity" to each of us as "the clear sign" in which we give ourselves to others.[63] "Thus, *human nature* must be understood on the basis of the *unity of body and soul*."[64]

"The denial of this duality not only erases the vision of human beings as the fruit of an act of creation but risks the idea of the human person as a sort of abstraction who 'chooses for himself what his nature is to be.'"[65] Hence, the *Catechism of the Catholic Church* declares that "*sexuality* affects all aspects of the human person in the unity of his body and soul" (*CCC* 2332).

---

[60] Ibid., no. 20.

[61] Ibid.

[62] Ibid., no. 22 (quoting Pope Francis, encyclical letter *Amoris Laetitia* (March 19, 2016), no. 34).

[63] Ibid., no. 32.

[64] Ibid.

[65] Ibid., no. 34.

This understanding of the body informs our understanding of the family. "The family is the natural place for the relationship of reciprocity and communion between man and woman to find its fullest realization."[66] That makes sense: the family is the context in which a man and woman can most freely give every part of themselves to the other: "For it is in the family that man and woman, united by a free and fully conscious *pact of conjugal love*, can live out 'a totality in which all the elements of the person enter.'"[67]

Indeed, that is the lesson the Church asks us to teach our children. Every child has the fundamental right to "grow up in a family with a father and a mother capable of creating a suitable environment for the child's development and emotional maturity."[68] And it "is precisely within the *nucleus of the family unit* that children can learn how to recognize the value and the beauty of the differences between the two sexes, along with their equal dignity, and their reciprocity at a biological, functional, psychological, and social level."[69] While we should recognize that not every individual forms a family, we also know that by design, each of us reflects the reality that we came from a family, and we each have a body designed to create a family, whether we do so or not.

Rejecting these truths about sex — including the associated truths about marriage — has promoted a dysfunctional notion of freedom and has caused great harm to families and children.[70]

Bishop Burbidge explains that dominating the body is related to dominating creation

We have been blessed with courageous American bishops who have taken the Congregation's thoughtful and complex ideas about human

66 Ibid., no. 36.
67 Ibid.
68 Ibid., no. 38.
69 Ibid.
70 Ibid., no. 43.

nature and sexuality and elaborated on them in very practical, easily understood terms. We'll begin with Arlington Bishop Michael Francis Burbidge, who in August 2021 issued *A Catechesis on the Human Person and Gender Ideology*. It beautifully summarizes everything we've discussed so far.

Bishop Burbidge begins by referencing the *Catechism of the Catholic Church* and explaining the three principles that undergird the Church's teachings about the human body:

> First, the human body is an "embodied soul," the composite of the spiritual and physical. The human soul is created to animate one particular body. To be a human person means to be a unity of body and soul from the moment of conception. Thus, the body reveals not only the soul, but the person; the person, as a unity of body and soul, acts through the body. Thus, each person's body, given by God from the moment of conception, is neither foreign nor a burden, but an integral part of the person.
>
> Second, and in keeping with the authoritative witness of Scripture (see Gen 1:27), the human person is created male or female. The human soul is created to animate and be embodied by one particular, specifically male or female, body. A person's sex is an immutable biological reality, determined at conception. The sexed body reveals God's design not only for each individual person, but also for all human beings, by "establishing us in a relationship with other living beings." ...
>
> It is important to note that there may be a variety of ways in which a person may express his or her sexual identity as male or female, according to the norms and practices of a particular time or culture. Moreover, a person may have atypical interests, but this does not change the person's sexual identity as either male or female.
>
> Third, the differences between man and woman are ordered towards their complementary union in marriage.

Indeed, the differences between man and woman, male and female, are unintelligible apart from such a union.[71]

Bishop Burbidge observes that "sexual difference is at the heart of family life." And "children need, and have a right to, a father and a mother" to the extent that is possible.[72]

Bishop Burbidge then describes the significance of these truths: "The body is not a limitation or confinement but one with the soul in the life of grace and glory to which the human person is called."[73] The Apostle Paul puts it well in his First Letter to the Corinthians: "Do you not know that your body is a temple of the Holy Spirit within you, whom you have from God? You are not your own, for you were bought with a price. So glorify God in your body" (1 Cor. 6:19–20).

Bishop Burbidge continues:

> Likewise, the relationship between man and woman as masculine and feminine has transcendent significance. Their complementary union serves as an icon of the marriage between Christ and the Church (see Eph. 5:31–32). Through procreation, spouses welcome new life into the world and become a community of persons that images the Trinity.[74]

In other words, when we reject our sex, or reject God's plan for marriage, we reject the family-as-icon-of-the-Trinity design that God ordained.

> Unfortunately, we experience our human nature not as the original harmony intended by the Creator but as fallen and wounded. One of the legacies of Original Sin is the disharmony and alienation between body and soul.

---

[71] Bishop Burbidge, *A Catechesis on the Human Person and Gender Ideology*, 2.
[72] Ibid., 3.
[73] Ibid.
[74] Ibid.

Immediately after sinning, Adam and Eve "sewed fig leaves together and made themselves aprons" (Gen 3:7). They evidenced their sense of alienation from their own bodies by seeking to conceal them. Everyone experiences this disharmony in various ways and to varying degrees. Nevertheless, it does not negate the profound oneness of the human person's body and soul.[75]

Bishop Burbidge notes that a "belief in a 'transgender' identity rejects the significance of the sexed body and seeks cultural, medical, and legal validation of the person's self-defined identity — an approach called 'gender affirmation.'" Yet "we know from biology that a person's sex is genetically determined at conception and present in every cell of the body. Because the body tells us about ourselves, our biological sex does in fact indicate our inalienable identity as male or female."[76] As a result of this conflict,

> so-called "transitioning" might change a person's appearance and physical traits (hormones, breasts, genitalia, etc.) but does not in fact change the truth of the person's identity as male or female, a truth reflected in every cell of the body. Indeed, no amount of "masculinizing" or "feminizing" hormones or surgery can make a man into a woman, or a woman into a man.
>
> The claim to "be transgender" or the desire to seek "transition" rests on a mistaken view of the human person, rejects the body as a gift from God, and leads to grave harm. To affirm someone in an identity at odds with biological sex or to affirm a person's desired "transition" is to mislead that person. It involves speaking and interacting with that person in an untruthful manner.[77]

[75] Ibid.
[76] Ibid., 4.
[77] Ibid.

Worse — and as we'll explore in more detail in subsequent chapters:

> There is ample evidence that "gender affirmation" not only does not resolve a person's struggles but also can in fact exacerbate them. The acceptance and/or approval of a person's claimed transgender identity is particularly dangerous in the case of children, whose psychological development is both delicate and incomplete. First and foremost, a child needs to know the truth: He or she has been created male or female, forever. Affirming a child's distorted self-perception or supporting a child's desire to "be" someone other than the person (male or female) God created, gravely misleads and confuses the child about "who" he or she is.[78]

Finally, "'gender-affirming' medical or surgical interventions cause significant, even irreparable, bodily harm to children and adolescents." Interventions including puberty blockers, cross-sex hormones, and surgery "involve serious mutilations of the human body, and are morally unacceptable."[79] And

> although some advocates justify "gender affirmation" as necessary to reduce the risk of suicide, such measures appear to offer only temporary psychological relief, and *suicidal risks remain significantly elevated following gender-transitioning measures....* Indeed, to disregard or withhold information about the harms of pursuing "transition" or about the benefits of alternative, psychotherapeutic treatments constitutes a failure in both justice and charity.[80]

[78] Ibid.
[79] Ibid.
[80] Ibid., 5; emphasis added.

Archbishop Carlson responds to gender ideology

Also expressing his love and care for the people he shepherds, St. Louis Archbishop Robert J. Carlson issued his *Compassion and Challenge: Reflections on Gender Ideology* in June 2020.[81] He takes the Church's teachings about the human body and authentic freedom and juxtaposes them against the motivating principles of gender ideology, pointing out the conflicts and inconsistencies.

Archbishop Carlson begins by defining the three philosophies that underlie the transgender movement. All three will sound similar to what we've been discussing: (1) "feelings define our identity" rather than our bodies, (2) "human integrity means acting on our persistent desires" rather than God's plan for us, and (3) "anyone who doesn't affirm our feelings and actions hates us." He encourages Catholics "to object to each of those ideas."[82]

First, Archbishop Carlson emphasizes that "feelings are a *part* of us but they do not *define* us." And that's a good thing! Feelings are always real, but they are not always true. They are fleeting and fickle things that do not always reflect reality and frequently change — especially in children. As the Archbishop puts it, if "we let our feelings define us we wouldn't have a stable identity at all!"[83]

Second, "human integrity requires us to *sift* our desires, not simply *follow* them." And that's for a simple reason:

> Our desires have many sources. Some of them are rooted in our identity as God's sons and daughters. Some are the result of original sin — our inherited fallen condition. Some come from our personal history of sin. Human experience

---

[81] Archbishop Robert J. Carlson, *Compassion and Challenge: Reflections on Gender Ideology* (June 1, 2020); available at https://www.archstl.org/Portals/0/Pastoral%20letters/Compassion%20and%20Challenge%20-%20letter%20size.pdf. https://perma.cc/SS2Q-QGHZ

[82] Ibid., 6.

[83] Ibid.

> tells us that following our desires sometimes helps us live
> well and sometimes leads to trouble.... Desires are not self-
> authenticating. Whether or not they move us toward
> Heaven is the criterion for making decisions.[84]

Sin is real, and the persistent existence of a desire — whether it is to overeat, consume too much alcohol, abuse our relationships with others, or to tell untruths — is no proof that "God made us this way."

Third, "disagreement is not hatred." As we've discussed, "to love is to will the good of another. If I love someone, then sometimes I need to speak out. Parents, coaches, teachers, siblings, and friends can respect our freedom even while saying: 'I don't think that's good for you. I don't see that bringing out the best in you.'"[85]

As Archbishop Carlson emphasizes:

> The Catholic faith teaches that [our] biological differences
> are profoundly meaningful. Sexual identity is written into
> every level of our physical being, from chromosomes to
> hormones to anatomy. We are called to integrate those re-
> alities into the psychological and spiritual aspect of our
> lives, not override them.[86]

What's more, Archbishop Carlson continues, human freedom is "not perfected simply in choosing freely. We can all name examples of people freely choosing something that's bad for them and bad for others. Freedom is perfected in the combination of choosing freely *and* choosing the good."[87] In chapter two, we discussed true freedom in the context of LeBron James and playing professional basketball. Archbishop Carlson uses the analogy of playing a musical instrument. "You don't have more freedom simply because you've never had lessons. You're

---

[84]   Ibid.
[85]   Ibid., 6–7.
[86]   Ibid., 7.
[87]   Ibid., 8; emphasis added.

most free to make beautiful music when you've been trained and learned discipline. The same is true for excellence in human living."[88]

Finally, Archbishop Carlson encourages all of us to respond to gender ideology with compassion without compromising the truth and what God wills to promote the flourishing of every individual. "Gender ideology wants us to meet people where they are, capitulate to their demands, and celebrate them as they are." In contrast, "Jesus calls us to meet people where they are, proclaim the truth of God's plan, and accompany them along the way of that plan."[89] He admonishes that "love always has two parts: compassion, and the challenging truth about God's plan. If we lack either — the compassion or the challenge — our love isn't fully Christian."[90]

Pope Francis speaks of the dangers of gender ideology

Pope Francis has also courageously addressed the dangers of gender ideology both in official papal documents and in less formal public statements. While emphatically encouraging us to support and accompany those who profess a "gender identity" that diverges from their biological sex, the pope has been equally firm about the need to do so in truth.

In *Amoris Laetitia* (The Joy of Love), his 2016 papal exhortation, Pope Francis explained that by denying "the difference and reciprocity in nature of a man and a woman" and promoting a "personal identity and emotional intimacy radically separated from the biological difference between male and female," gender ideology reduces human identity to "the choice of the individual" and undermines the "anthropological basis of the family."[91] He continues:

---

[88] Ibid.
[89] Ibid.
[90] Ibid., 12.
[91] Pope Francis, *Amoris Laetitia*, no. 56.

It is one thing to be understanding of human weakness and the complexities of life, and another to accept ideologies that attempt to sunder what are inseparable aspects of reality. Let us not fall into the sin of trying to replace the Creator.[92]

Pope Francis then elaborates on what he means by this:

We are creatures, and not omnipotent. Creation is prior to us and must be received as a gift. At the same time, we are called to protect our humanity, and this means, in the first place, accepting it and respecting it *as it was created*.[93]

In other words, just like our age, our height, and our other natural, bodily characteristics, our sex is an objective gift from God, not a subjective choice that we should manipulate and try to change in a way that rejects the gift.

Pope Francis emphasized the need to accept God's gift of our bodies in his 2015 encyclical letter *Laudato Si'* (Care for Our Common Home), noting that nothing less than our humanity is at stake. "Pope Benedict XVI spoke of an 'ecology of man' based on the fact that man too has a nature that he must respect and that he cannot manipulate at will." As a result,

Acceptance of our bodies as God's gift is vital for welcoming and accepting the entire world as a gift from the Father and our common home, whereas thinking that we enjoy absolute power over our own bodies turns, often subtly, into thinking that we enjoy absolute power over creation. Learning to accept our body, to care for it and to

92 Ibid.
93 Ibid.

respect its fullest meaning, is an essential element of any genuine human ecology.[94]

Pope Francis then went on to explain that acceptance of God's gift of our maleness and femaleness is critical to happiness:

> Valuing one's own body in its femininity or masculinity is necessary if I am going to be able to recognize myself in an encounter with someone who is different. In this way we can joyfully accept the specific gifts of another man or woman, the work of God the Creator, and find mutual enrichment. It is not a healthy attitude which would seek "to cancel out sexual difference."[95]

Indeed, the issue of transgenderism has assumed such importance in contemporary Western culture that Pope Francis also used a 2015 general audience address to emphasize the importance of male and female complementarity, what it means for understanding ourselves and others, and the negative consequences of gender ideology:

> As we all know, sexual difference is present in so many forms of life, on the great scale of living beings. But man and woman alone are made in the image and likeness of God: the biblical text repeats it three times in two passages.... This tells us that it is not man alone who is the image of God or woman alone who is the image of God, but man and woman *as a couple* who are the image of God. The difference between man and woman is not meant to stand in opposition, or to subordinate, but is for the sake of communion and generation, always in the image and likeness of God.
>
> Experience teaches us: in order to know oneself well and develop harmoniously, a human being *needs* the

---

[94]   Pope Francis, *Laudato Si'*, no. 155.
[95]   Ibid.

reciprocity of man and woman. When that is lacking, one can see the consequences.... We can say that without the mutual enrichment of this relationship — in thought and in action, in affection and in work, as well as in faith — the two cannot even understand the depth of what it means to be man and woman.[96]

Pope Francis then gets down to brass tacks: "Modern contemporary culture has opened new spaces, new forms of freedom, and new depths in order to enrich the understanding of this difference. But it has also introduced many doubts and much skepticism." That is why Pope Francis asks himself "if the so-called gender theory is not, at the same time, an expression of frustration and resignation, which seeks to cancel out sexual difference because it no longer knows how to confront it." Pope Francis rejects gender ideology in favor of better — and more human, move loving — relationships:

> The removal of difference in fact creates a problem, not a solution. In order to resolve the problems in their relationships, men and women need to speak to one another more, listen to each other more, get to know one another better, love one another more. They must treat each other with respect and cooperate in friendship.[97]

When men and women do this, Pope Francis insists, "sustained by the grace of God, it is possible to plan a lifelong marital and family union. The marital and familial bond is a serious matter, and it is so for everyone, not just for believers." And he urges "intellectuals not to leave this theme aside, as if it had to become secondary in order to foster a more free and just society."[98] And so Pope Francis exhorts that the

---

[96] Pope Francis, General Audience, St. Peter's Square (April 15, 2015).
[97] Ibid.
[98] Ibid.

great responsibility of the Church, of all believers, and first of all of believing families, which derives from us, impels people to rediscover the beauty of the creative design that also inscribes the image of God in the alliance between man and woman.... Jesus encourages us explicitly to bear witness to this beauty, which is the image of God.[99]

Pope Francis returned to these themes in two interviews surrounding his tenth anniversary as pope. He maintained that there is a difference between pastoral outreach and accepting "gender ideology," which he warned "is one of the most dangerous ideological colonizations."[100] "Why is it dangerous?" he asked. "Because it dilutes differences, and the richness of men and women and of all humanity is the tension of differences. It is to grow through the tension of differences."[101] A theory of gender that views being male or female as a choice or social construct instead of a fact related to biological identity "is diluting the differences and making the world the same, all blunt, all equal," he concluded, "and that goes against the human vocation."[102]

Bishop Donald E. DeGrood of the Sioux Falls Diocese sums up these teachings in a beautiful way:

> As Pope Francis notes, we must always respect the sacred dignity of each individual person, but that does not mean the Church must accept the confused notions of gender ideology. We must not demean or deny the sincerity and struggle of those who experience same-sex attraction or who feel his/her true gender identity is different from his/her biological sex. Rather, we seek to accompany

[99] Ibid.
[100] Cindy Wooden, " 'Fraternity, Tears, Smiles': Pope Shares Hopes for the Future," *USCCB*, March 13, 2023, https://www.usccb.org/news/2023/fraternity-tears-smiles-pope-shares-hopes-future. https://perma.cc/HWV8-BDU2
[101] Ibid.
[102] Ibid.

them on their journey of life, offering them the light of the Gospel as they try to find their way forward.

These truths are not merely faith based; rather, such realities are also knowable through the use of properly functioning senses and right reason (Pope St. John Paul II, *Fides et Ratio*, no. 22). We do not serve anyone's greater good by falsifying the truth, for it is only the truth that frees us for the full life that God offers to each of us. Thus, when a person experiences same-sex attraction or some form of gender dysphoria, such struggles do not change the biological fact of how God created that person, and it would be untruthful for the Catholic Church or our Catholic schools to pretend otherwise.[103]

In sum, there is great beauty in these many reflections of Church leaders on human sexuality and gender ideology, truths that go to the essence of what it means to be a person. That is why the Church teaches that every person should accept her or his sexual identity, particularly in the face of theories that "gender identity" is a psychological or "cultural and social product."[104] Yet the critics persist, rebuking those who rely on the Bible, faith, and reason as individuals who deny the scientific research behind gender ideology. So let's look at the scientific research next.

---

[103] Bishop Donald E. DeGrood, *Diocesan Policy: Conforming with the Church's Teaching on Human Sexuality in Education Settings* (July 1, 2022); available at https://s3.documentcloud.org/documents/22131508/bishop-ogorman-policy.pdf. https://perma.cc/VV8H-6VMY

[104] Pontifical Council for Justice and Peace, *Compendium of the Social Doctrine of the Church* (2004), no. 224.

CHAPTER 4

What Does Scientific Inquiry
Say about Gender Ideology?

IN A LETTER FROM 1988, Pope St. John Paul II wrote, "Science can purify religion from error and superstition; religion can purify science from idolatry and false absolutes." The relationship between the two, he explained, is necessary: "For the truth of the matter is that the Church and the scientific community will inevitably interact; their options do not include isolation."[105]

Critics of the Church and the Church's teachings sometimes accuse the Church of ignoring scientific investigation (see appendix two). Indeed, transgender advocates sometimes say that there is a consensus among doctors and scientists that sex is merely a societal construct and that "gender identity" is a better indicator of someone's nature than their so-called "sex assigned at birth." But in fact, scientific

---

[105] Pope St. John Paul II, "Letter to Reverend George V. Coyne, S.J., Director of the Vatican Observatory" (June 1, 1988), https://www.vatican.va/content/john-paul-ii/en/letters/1988/documents/hf_jp-ii_let_19880601_padre-coyne.html. https://perma.cc/TEQ4-9JWE

inquiry shows the exact opposite. There is actually no *scientific* basis for an individual having a "gender identity" that is different than their biological sex, only abstract philosophical speculation. So scientific inquiry and the Church are in complete agreement.

Even after a so-called gender "reassignment" surgery, every cell in a person's body is still coded with chromosomes that will tell any scientist whether that person is male or female. In other words, sex is a physiological reality. That is why a recent paper by the American College of Pediatricians on gender dysphoria (GD) in children agrees with the Church: "GD is a problem that resides in the mind not in the body. Children with GD do not have a disordered body — even though they feel as if they do."[106] It is simply biologically false to say that a boy was born in a girl's body or vice versa.

The difference between boys and girls is not just physical

Pope St. John Paul II beautifully recognized that differences between males and females are more than just physical. In 1995, he wrote a *Letter to Women* in which he discussed the feminine genius. He began with a series of thank-yous. The pope thanked "women who are mothers" for having sheltered their children in the womb, guiding their child's first steps, and serving as "the anchor as the child makes its way along the journey of life." He thanked "women who are wives" for engaging "in a relationship of mutual giving, at the service of love and life."[107]

Next, the pope praised "women who are daughters and women who are sisters" for bringing to their families and to society "the richness of your sensitivity, your intuitiveness, your generosity and fidelity." He thanked "women who work" for making "an indispensable contribution to the growth of a culture which unites reason

---

[106] Michelle Cretella, "Gender Dysphoria in Children," *American College of Pediatricians*, November 2018, https://acpeds.org/position-statements/gender-dysphoria-in-children. https://perma.cc/645L-MWSQ

[107] Pope St. John Paul II, *Letter to Women* (June 29, 1995).

and feeling." He expressed appreciation for "consecrated women" for opening themselves "with obedience and fidelity to the gift of God's love" and for helping "the Church and all mankind to experience a 'spousal' relationship to God." And he thanked "every woman" for enriching "the world's understanding and help[ing] to make human relations more honest and authentic." Then, after recapitulating God's design of creating man and woman in the Book of Genesis, the pope praised the many virtues of women, in particular, how "women *acknowledge the person*, because they see persons with their hearts."[108]

The difference between men and women is not mere religious teaching; it also comports with what scientific research has shown. "After the reproductive organs, the brain is possibly the most 'sexed' organ in a human being."[109] This doesn't mean there are "male brains" and there are "female brains." But "on average there are differences in the brains of males and females that tend to make a difference in how men and women experience emotion and pain, how they see and hear, and how they remember and navigate."[110]

In fact, as reported by a neurobiologist after a literature review, there are "a surge of findings that highlight the influence of sex on many areas of cognition and behavior, including memory, emotion, vision, hearing, the processing of faces, and the brain's response to stress hormones."[111] There is "abundant evidence" demonstrating

[108] Ibid.

[109] Ryan T. Anderson, *When Harry Became Sally: Responding to the Transgender Moment* (New York: Encounter Books, 2018), 84.

[110] Ibid.

[111] Larry Cahill, "His Brain, Her Brain," *Scientific American*, October 1, 2012, https://www.scientificamerican.com/article/his-brain-her-brain-2012-10-23/. https://perma.cc/8HTF-H946

that "sex influences on brain function are ubiquitous, found at every level of neuroscience."[112]

As a society, we have always recognized these innate differences without difficulty. In a wildly popular book published in 1992, American author and relationship counselor John Gray argued that *Men Are from Mars, Women Are from Venus*. The book sold 6.6 million copies and finished as the "highest ranked work of nonfiction" from the 1990s.[113] Gray made the case that many common relational problems among men and women stem from the sexes' psychological differences. He claimed that men and women could be best understood by the distinctive ways they respond to stressful situations, and the book's title became a cultural meme that millions of people quickly adopted.

Of course, not every boy conforms to societal stereotypes about what it means to be "male," nor does every girl conform to societal stereotypes about being "female." But scientific research strongly suggests that we should not blindly accept the claims of gender activists that gender norms are *all* just social constructs and therefore meaningless.

In fact, there's a glaring hypocrisy to this claim. On the one hand, gender activists say that social norms for males and females are made up and don't have to be followed. Men do not have to be stoic; they can be tender and compassionate. Women do not have to be emotional; they can have nerves of steel. At the same time, these activists argue that if you "feel" like the opposite sex, then you must do everything you can — up to and including major

---

[112] Larry Cahill, "A Half-Truth Is a Whole Lie: On the Necessity of Investigating Sex Influences on the Brain," *Endocrinology* 153, no. 6 (June 2012): 2542.

[113] "Grisham Ranks as Top-Selling Author of Decade," *CNN.com*, December 31, 1999. See https://web.archive.org/web/20120908181659/http://articles.cnn.com/1999-12-31/entertainment/1990.sellers_1_book-sales-cumulative-sales-copies?_s=PM:books. https://perma.cc/28GD-L6H9

reconstructive surgery — so that your body will fit the stereotype for the opposite sex that you have in your head. There is no way to reconcile these competing claims.

The reality is that "sex is a bodily, biological reality, and gender is how we give social expression to that reality. Gender properly understood is a social manifestation of human nature, *springing forth from biological realities*, though shaped by rational moral choice."[114] To put it another way, "gender is socially shaped, but it is not a mere social construct. It originates in biology, but in turn it directs our bodily nature to higher human goods."[115]

A person's "gender identity" does not establish his or her sex

As noted above, "sex" and "gender" are considered two distinct categories by many today. While "sex" is binary and objective, determined by one's chromosomal constitution and ultimately by clearly defined reproductive capacities, gender activists say that "gender" is a subjective sense of identity, a social role generated by cultural norms.

The central, underlying basis for sex is the distinction between the reproductive roles of males and females.[116] In biology, an organism is male or female if it is biologically and physiologically designed to perform one of the respective roles in sexual reproduction.[117] Sex is the "biological indication of male and female (understood in the context of reproductive capacity), such as sex chromosomes, gonads, sex hormones, and nonambiguous internal and external genitalia."[118]

---

[114] Anderson, *When Harry Became Sally*, 149.

[115] Ibid.

[116] Lawrence S. Mayer and Paul R. McHugh, "Executive Summary," *Sexuality and Gender: Findings from the Biological, Psychological, and Social Sciences*, *The New Atlantis*, no. 50 (Fall 2016): 7–9.

[117] Ibid.; see also "Female," *Oxford Dictionary of Biology*, 7th ed. (Oxford: Oxford University Press, 2015); "Male," ibid.

[118] American Psychiatric Association, *Diagnostic and Statistical Manual of Mental Disorders*, 5th ed. ("DSM-5") (2013), 829.

This makes sex innate and immutable; it cannot be changed. The genetic information directing development of male or female reproductive organs and other primary sexual traits, which normally is encoded on chromosome pairs "XY" and "XX," is present immediately at the moment of conception. As early as eight weeks gestation, a baby's internally produced sex hormones cause prenatal imprinting that ultimately influences behaviors after birth.[119] And while the reproductive system serves as a virtually infallible identifier of one's sex, *every cell in the body containing a nucleus is marked with a sexual identity by its chromosomal constitution: XX or XY.* Accordingly, sex is not "assigned" at birth but established at conception; it "declares itself anatomically in utero and is acknowledged at birth."[120] Sex is a phenomenon that is verified; it is a scientific fact.

The same cannot be said of gender, which, as just discussed above, reflects how much a boy or girl conforms to or deviates from socially normative behavior for young males or females. Unfortunately for gender ideologists, there is no objective, scientific definition for what it means to "behave like" a boy or a girl. It is not scientifically verifiable at all. Moreover, what is considered gender-typical behavior for males and females changes over time within a given culture and varies among cultures.

[119] Francisco I. Reyes, J. S. D. Winter, C. Faiman, "Studies on Human Sexual Development. I. Fetal Gonadal and Adrenal Sex Steroids," *The Journal of Clinical Endocrinology and Metabolism* 37, no. 1 (July 1, 1973): 74–78; Michael Lombardo et al., "Fetal Testosterone Influences Sexually Dimorphic Gray Matter in the Human Brain," *Journal of Neuroscience* 32, no. 2 (January 11, 2012): 674–680; P. C. Sizonenko, "Human Sexual Differentiation," *Geneva Foundation for Medical Education and Research*, 2017, https://www.gfmer.ch/Books/Reproductive_health/Human_sexual_differentiation.htm. https://perma.cc/W87G-XXZM

[120] Michelle A. Cretella, "Gender Dysphoria in Children and Suppression of Debate," *Journal of American Physicians and Surgeons* 21, no. 2 (Summer 2016): 51.

For example, it surprises many to learn that in the early 1900s, pink was a popular color for boys and blue for girls. As the 1918 trade publication *Earnshaw's Infants' Department* explained, the "generally accepted rule is pink for the boys, and blue for the girls. The reason is that pink, being a more decided and stronger color, is more suitable for the boy, while blue, which is more delicate and dainty, is prettier for the girl."[121]

In addition to changing cultural expectations, a child's interests can change over time too. For example, a girl who behaves like a "tomboy" may modify her behavior as she ages, and a boy who prefers quiet play imitating home life may develop an interest in adventure, sports, or hunting later on. Unlike sex, then, which is fixed, gender is something of "a free-floating artifice."[122]

The concept of "gender identity disorder" is one that psychiatrists and psychologists have long held. A person with this condition experiences a sense of disharmony or "dysphoria" between the gender expectations associated with her or his biological sex and her or his biological sex itself.[123] Boys may subjectively feel as if they are girls, and girls may subjectively feel as if they are boys — according to *their own sense* of what the feeling of being a member of the opposite sex must be like.[124] As explained by one of the primary manuals for assessment and diagnosis of mental disorders, the DSM-5 (*The Diagnostic and Statistical Manual of Mental Disorders*, fifth edition), "transgender refers to the

---

[121] Cydney Grannan, "Has Pink Always Been a 'Girly' Color?" *Britannica*, https://www.britannica.com/story/has-pink-always-been-a-girly-color. https://perma.cc/PC79-L8HB

[122] Judith Butler, *Gender Trouble: Feminism and the Subversion of Identity* (New York: Routledge, 1990), 6–7. Butler is a gender studies writer who has controversially argued that sex itself is a construct.

[123] Tomer Shechner, "Gender Identity Disorder: A Literature Review from a Developmental Perspective," *Israel Journal of Psychiatry and Related Science* 47, no. 2 (2010): 132–138.

[124] American Psychiatric Association, DSM-5, 452.

broad spectrum of individuals who transiently or persistently identify with a gender different from their natal [birth] gender."[125]

Dysphoria may also manifest with males or females claiming an array of nonbinary genders — or no gender at all. Some "gender-queer" people "identify their gender as falling outside the binary constructs of 'male' and 'female,'" and instead choose other gender identities, such as "androgynous, multigendered, gender noncon-forming, third gender, and two-spirit."[126]

But subjective feelings, strong as they may be, neither are nor change objective reality. As one expert puts it, "This 'alternate per-spective' of an 'innate gender fluidity' arising from prenatally 'femi-nized' or 'masculinized' brains trapped in the wrong body is an ideological belief *that has no basis in rigorous science.*"[127] Indeed, there is no scientific basis for the belief that men who identify as women actually *are* women "trapped" in men's bodies.[128]

Significantly, studies of brain structure and function have not demonstrated any conclusive biological basis for transgendered identity.[129] Some researchers believe that transgenderism may be

---

[125] Ibid., 451. It is curious, and unexplained, that the DSM uses the word "gender" twice in this definition rather than contrasting gender with "natal sex."

[126] American Psychiatric Association, *Answers to Your Questions*, 2.

[127] Cretella, "Gender Dysphoria in Children," 51.

[128] J. Michael Bailey and Kiira Triea, "What Many Transgender Activists Don't Want You to Know: And Why You Should Know it Anyway," *Perspectives in Biology and Medicine* 50, no. 4 (Fall 2007): 521–534.

[129] For more on brain structure, see: Giuseppina Rametti et al., "White Matter Microstructure in Female to Male Transsexuals Before Cross-Sex Hormonal Treatment. A Diffusion Tensor Imaging Study," *Journal of Psychiatric Research* 45, no. 2 (February 2011): 199–204.

For more information on brain activity, see: Emiliano Santarnec-chi et al., "Intrinsic Cerebral Connectivity Analysis in an Untreated Fe-male-to-Male Transsexual Subject: A First Attempt Using Resting-State fMRI," *Neuroendocrinology* 96, no. 3 (September 2012): 188–93; and Hans Berglund et al., "Male-to-Female Transsexuals Show Sex-Atypical Hypothalamus Activation When Smelling Odorous Steroids," *Cerebral Cortex* 18, no. 8 (August 2008): 1900–1908.

attributed to other biological causes, such as hormone exposure in utero.[130] But no existing scientific evidence supports that conclusion.

The result of all this is that, medically speaking, "there are no laboratory, imaging, or other objective tests to diagnose a 'true transgender' child."[131] In other words, a gender-dysphoric girl is not — scientifically speaking — a girl trapped in a boy's body, or vice versa. Furthermore, individuals retain their sex no matter their beliefs about their gender. And it is not loving to treat gender activists' dishonesty about these matters as though it were the truth.

Doesn't the existence of disorders of sexual development prove that sex is not binary?

Proponents of transgender ideology will often point to disorders of sexual development — people who are born with indeterminate or intermediate sex characteristics — as the basis for claiming that sex is not actually binary but exists on a spectrum. For example, an infamous illustration in a 2017 *Scientific American* article plotted this condition as one point on a continuous axis that moved from "typical female" to "typical male."[132]

But such an argument is based on a misunderstanding (or deliberate misrepresentation) of what some call the "intersex" condition,

---

[130] See Nancy Segal, "Two Monozygotic Twin Pairs Discordant for Female-to-Male Transsexualism," *Archives of Sexual Behavior* 35, no. 3 (June 2006): 347–358.

[131] Michael K. Laidlaw et al., letter to the editor, "Endocrine Treatment of Gender-Dysphoric/Gender-Incongruent Persons: An Endocrine Society Clinical Practice Guideline," *The Journal of Clinical Endocrinology and Metabolism* 104, no. 3 (March 2019): 686–687.

[132] Amanda Montañez, "Visualizing Sex as a Spectrum," *Scientific American*, August 29, 2017, https://blogs.scientificamerican.com/sa-visual/visualizing-sex-as-a-spectrum/. https://perma.cc/4FB3-2WVL

which is a disorder of sexual development, or DSD, that occurs in about 1 in 5,000 births.[133] These disorders have many causes, including chromosomal abnormalities and genetic mutations. Those with Klinefelter syndrome have XXY chromosomes. Those with Turner syndrome have a single X chromosome (rather than XX or XY). And so on.

If the subject was disorders of any other part or system of the body, there would not even be a discussion about the topic. For example, someone born with a kidney defect does not have a "different kind of kidney." They have a disordered kidney. Someone with a heart defect does not have a "second kind of heart" but a diseased heart. The fact that someone is born with a faulty circulatory system does not prove there is a "spectrum" of normal circulatory systems. As Ryan Anderson explains it, "organs are judged healthy or sick on the basis of how they perform their function within the system of which they are a part."[134] There is no such thing as a third sex, much less a sex spectrum.[135]

To further advance the false proposition of sex as a spectrum, some will say that people with disorders of sexual development make up 1–2 percent of the population, and that the condition is "as common as red hair."[136] This is demonstrably false. The actual, documented figure is 0.018 percent of the population.[137] Regardless, just

[133] Peter A. Lee et al., "Global Disorders of Sex Development Update since 2006: Perceptions, Approach and Care," *Hormone Research in Paediatrics* 85, no. 3 (2016): 159.

[134] Ryan T. Anderson, *When Harry Became Sally: Responding to the Transgender Moment* (New York: Encounter Books, 2018): 92.

[135] The 2015 revision of the consensus statement of the Intersex Society of North America does *not* endorse DSDs as a third sex. Declaration of Quentin L. Van Meter, M.D., U.S. District Court, Middle District of North Carolina, Case 1:16-cv-00425-TDS-JEP, Exhibit I.

[136] Colin Wright, "Intersex Is Not As Common as Red Hair," *Reality's Last Stand*, December 7, 2020, https://www.realityslaststand.com/p/intersex-is-not-as-common-as-red. https://perma.cc/4DM7-JRFZ

[137] Ibid. (Citing Leonard Sax, "How Common Is Intersex? A Response to Anne Fausto-Sterling," *Journal of Sex Research* 39, no. 3 (August 2002): 174–178).

because the rare person's physical sex characteristics at a macro level (as opposed to a cellular level) might be ambiguous does not mean that sex for the human population as a whole is not binary. The theory of a sex spectrum is "a false theory of biology that distorts human nature and harms vulnerable individuals,"[138] the exact opposite of truth that helps every individual to grow into who God designed them to be.

In sum, both the Church and scientific inquiry are clear that someone's self-professed "gender identity" does not define their sex any more than a person's self-professed height or race defines those characteristics. But if that's the case, then what *is* a transgender person's "identity"? Or anyone's identity for that matter? That is the subject to which we will turn next.

---

[138] Colin Wright, "Sex Is Not a Spectrum," *Reality's Last Stand*, February 1, 2021, https://www.realityslaststand.com/p/sex-is-not-a-spectrum. https://perma.cc/KT77-43G4

CHAPTER 5

What Is My Identity?

♀ ♂

Pope Benedict explains, "Each of us is the result of a thought of God. Each of us is willed, each of us is loved, each of us is necessary."[139] God's love gives us our identity. This identity defines our destiny: to know God, to love Him, and to serve Him in this world, and to be happy with Him forever in the next.[140]

The LGBTQ movement has redefined the meaning of the word "identity." Large segments of the population do not identify themselves as sons or daughters of God but as "gay," "lesbian," "pansexual," "nonbinary," "genderqueer," or one of many dozens of other sexual orientations and gender identities.

But it is not possible to reduce a person's identity simply to their sexual attractions, or to their sense of "gender" — at least, not for a Christian. Sexual attraction and our own sense of gender do not give us our identity; our identity comes from the fact that God loves us. It

---

[139] Pope Benedict XVI, "Inaugural Homily" (April 24, 2005).
[140] "Lesson First: On the End of Man, Question and Answer 6," *Baltimore Catechism No. 1.*

is a distortion of the human person to identify as "gay" or "nonbinary" or even "straight." "Your identity is something else, something profound," says Fr. Michael Schmitz. "You are a son or daughter of God. Your destiny is to live in Him."[141]

Our identity is not defined by our experiences or family history

Fr. Schmitz's book, *Made for Love: Same-Sex Attraction and the Catholic Church*, is a beautiful reflection on human sexuality, and chapter seven, regarding "identity," is a masterpiece. He begins with a difficult story about "Melanie," who was abused when she was just a child and in fact was herself conceived as the result of an assault. In Fr. Schmitz's words, "Melanie experienced herself as broken, used, and unlovable," someone who "did not see her life as having any kind of destination, any kind of real purpose."[142]

Yet someone introduced Melanie to Jesus Christ when she was twenty-four years old, and her life was transformed. Indeed! "Melanie is now a religious sister who travels around the country speaking to young men and women about the truth of *their* origin, *their* story, and *their* destiny."[143] Her experience as a victim of abuse did not define her identity as a daughter of God.

Some believe that their identity is defined by their family of origin, but that is also wrong. Think about the many poor decisions in Jesus' family tree, the House of David — from Abraham passing off his wife Sarah as his "sister," to Jacob lying to his father to steal the family blessing, to David and his adultery with Bathsheba and murder of her husband, Uriah. Yet Jesus' identity did not change because of his damaged family.

---

[141] Fr. Michael Schmitz, *Made for Love: Same-Sex Attraction and the Catholic Church* (San Francisco: Ignatius Press, 2017), 83.

[142] Ibid., 73–74.

[143] Ibid., 74.

So what does Pope Benedict mean when he says that "each of us is the result of a thought of God. Each of us is willed, each of us is loved, each of us is necessary"?[144] Fr. Schmitz answers that question: "Pope Benedict is saying that despite the situations of your birth, or whatever you may have been told about your origin ... your origin is the result of God's love. Your origin is love. Love is what gives you your identity."[145]

In the same way that we are not defined by our family or its history, we are not defined by our experiences. It's not uncommon when we meet someone to ask what they do. "I'm a lawyer." "I'm a football player." "I'm a mechanic." But the fact that we have experience in a particular occupation or hobby does not define our identity.

Think again about the example of Melanie. Once upon a time, she believed that her traumatic and painful experiences defined her identity. But she was wrong. And when she figured out who she was, it was as though she became an entirely different person.

Sometimes we choose our experiences. Sometimes, as in Melanie's case, those experiences happen even though we don't choose them. It doesn't matter. That is because our experiences do not define who we are or what choices we may make in the future. While experiences shape us, they are not our identity.

Our identity is not defined by our sexual attractions or perceived gender

Fr. John Harvey founded Courage, the Catholic apostolate that helps men and women who experience same-sex attraction to live happy and holy lives in accord with the teachings of the Church. Fr. Harvey connected the dots between mistakenly conflating our everyday experiences with our identity and mistakenly conflating our *sexual* experiences with our identity:

---

[144] Pope Benedict XVI, "Inaugural Homily" (April 24, 2005).

[145] Fr. Michael Schmitz, *Made for Love*, 76.

Imagine a fifteen-year-old boy and his buddy behind a shed, who out of curiosity smoked some cigarettes. If you busted them, you probably wouldn't identify them as smokers. But imagine the same fifteen-year-old boy going behind the shed with the same buddy, but instead of smoking, they experiment sexually with each other. Our culture responds affirmatively, saying, "Oh! You've discovered you're gay. That's *who you are*."[146]

But we shouldn't respond so differently to these situations. Smoking did not define the teenage boys' identity any more than the sexual experimentation did. Both situations involved poor choices; neither experience established an overarching identity like that of being a child of God.

It's not just the Church that sees this reality. The sex researcher Alfred Kinsey decried categorizing people who engaged in same-sex erotic activity as "being homosexual." He found that such labeling was confusing feelings and experiences with identity:

> It would encourage clearer thinking on these matters if persons were not characterized as heterosexual or homosexual but as individuals who have had certain amounts of heterosexual experience and certain amounts of homosexual experience. Instead of using these terms as substantives *which stand for persons*, or even as adjectives to describe persons, they may better be used to describe the nature of overt sexual relations, or of the stimuli to which an individual erotically responds.[147]

[146] Ibid., 77.

[147] A. C. Kinsey, W. R. Pomeroy, and C. E. Martin, *Sexual Behavior in the Human Male* (Philadelphia: W. B. Saunders, 1948), 656; quoted in Daniel C. Mattson, *Why I Don't Call Myself Gay* (San Francisco: Ignatius Press, 2017), 132; emphasis added.

There are two basic problems with the modern approach to identity that our culture emphasizes. First, we're extraordinarily bad at self-defining our own identity based on our experiences because we lack objectivity and tend to exaggerate in both directions. A fifth grader who gets straight A's in nearly all subjects but earns a B in math might believe she's "bad at math," and she would likely be wrong — many who are "good" at math receive Bs in advanced math classes, and sometimes academic performance is more a reflection of teaching or circumstances than innate ability. Consider other subjective viewpoints of ourselves: "I'm the best at relating to other people"; "I can never do anything right"; "I'm always the life of the party." Likely, every one of these self-assessments is grievously wrong, or at least over-exaggerated, and does not accurately define who we are.

Second, as we just discussed, our experiences and attractions do not determine our ultimate identity. Again, Fr. Schmitz says: "Having a homosexual or heterosexual attraction might be part of your experience, and a significant part no doubt. But is this your identity? No."[148] He continues:

> The truth revealed to us by Christ makes clear that your sexual orientation is not what ultimately defines you.... If we allow ourselves to be defined by our sexual attractions, we are reducing ourselves and defining ourselves by something far too small.[149]

And if we allow others to be defined by their sexual attractions or feelings about gender, we are not acting in their best interests. We are not really loving them.

So why has the use of labels based on sexual experiences and feelings, such as "gay" and "lesbian," become so popular to define

[148] Fr. Michael Schmitz, *Made for Love*, 79.
[149] Ibid., 78–79.

people? Because people do not hesitate to criticize and correct with respect to experiences ("Stop smoking!") or even feelings ("Get over it"!) — but they are loathe to criticize someone's identity, because to attack identity is to attack a person rather than an abstract idea.

Indeed, it was a tremendous accomplishment of the gay-rights movement to persuade culture to *think* about sexual orientation in terms of "identity." As gay-rights activist Dennis Altman wrote less than fifteen years after the raid of a gay bar that led to the 1969 Stonewall riots, "The greatest single victory of the gay movement over the past decade has been to shift the debate *from behavior to identity*."[150] And while Mr. Altman is tragically wrong about reality, he's undoubtedly correct about the success of the public-relations campaign.

But the conflation of gender preferences and our identity is even more damaging because there is in fact a significant overlap between the types of things that males and females like to do. To the extent that gender activists claim that a boy *is* a girl, what they're saying is that the boy thinks of himself in terms of the *stereotypes* of how he believes (or how others believe) a girl should dress, behave, and feel. And such gross stereotypes should never become labels for what makes us male and female, because they limit our understanding about ourselves and what males and females can do or accomplish. (True love — willing the good of the other — requires actions based on truth, not on fictitious stereotypes.)

Consider this graph from the Person and Identity website, an initiative of the Catholic Women's Forum at the Ethics and Public Policy Center:[151]

---

[150] Dennis Altman, *The Homosexualization of America* (Boston: Beacon Press, 1982), 42–43; quoted in Mattson, *Why I Don't Call Myself Gay*, 133.

[151] "FAQs: What about a person who has interests, preferences, or behaviors typically associated with the opposite sex?" *Person and Identity: A Project of the Catholic Women's Forum at the Ethics and Public Policy Center*, https://personandidentity.com/the-basics/#faqs. https://perma.cc/J65G-NN32

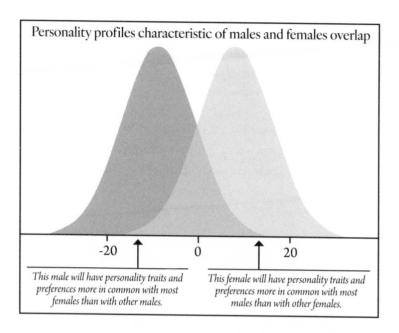

The graph maps the results of an international study of male and female personality traits in countries where people are free to embrace their preferences and interests. It shows that "personality and behavior do not define one's sex." Rather, a child of one sex who engages in behaviors and expresses preferences that stereotypically belong to the opposite sex "simply exists at the bend of a behavioral spectrum, and 'sex-atypical' behavior is part of the natural variation exhibited both within and between the sexes."[152]

In fact, based on the graph's distribution, we should *expect* stereotype busters:

> There are approximately forty million children in the United States between the ages of four and fourteen. The

---

[152] William J. Malone, Colin M. Wright, and Julia D. Robertson, "No One Is Born in 'The Wrong Body,'" *Quillette*, September 24, 2019, https://quillette.com/2019/09/24/no-one-is-born-in-the-wrong-body/. https://perma.cc/AJW8-DMK9

distribution curve above would suggest that roughly four million of them have personality profiles that are "sex atypical" but which are still part of the *natural distribution* of personalities within each sex.[153]

And as we'll be discussing in the next chapter, "telling a child that he or she was born in the wrong body pathologizes 'gender non-conforming' behavior and makes gender dysphoria less likely to resolve."[154]

Our identity is defined by our destiny

So if we're not identified by our family history, our experiences, our occupation, our sexual attractions, or our gender expression, what is our identity? It has everything to do with the purpose for which we were made. Our destiny. Again, Fr. Schmitz says:

> Jesus has revealed to all of us that we have a destination, a reason for existence that goes beyond *this* existence, this life.... Jesus further reveals that our destiny is love. Your destiny is to live forever in your Father's house.[155]

Now that's an identity worth getting excited about! And we live out this destiny through our bodies, which God created male and female.

To explain this understanding of our destiny, Fr. Schmitz turns to the Parable of the Prodigal Son in Luke's Gospel (Luke 15:11–32). You probably know the story. A successful man has two sons. The younger son demands his half of the inheritance immediately so he can leave the family estate and live freely, as he wants to live. His father gives his son the inheritance, and the son squanders the whole thing, engaging in "reckless living." Things are so bad that the son

---

153 Ibid.
154 Ibid.
155 Fr. Michael Schmitz, *Made for Love*, 79.

gets a job feeding pigs and longs to eat the pigs' food because they're being fed better than he. The son has lost all sense of who he is.

Then the son "came to himself" (Luke 15:17). He remembers that he is the son of a loving father. He resolves to go back home, admit that he has sinned against God and against his father, and consent to being treated as one of his father's hired servants. He sets off to confess, and the father, seeing his son coming from a distance, "felt compassion, and ran and embraced him and kissed him" (Luke 15:20). After his son apologizes and says he is "no longer worthy to be called your son," the father instructs his servants to "quickly" bring and put "the best robe" on his son and to place a ring on his finger and shoes on his feet. Then the father instructs that the fattened calf be killed for a celebration, "For this my son was dead, and is alive again; he was lost, and is found" (Luke 15:21–24).

Fr. Schmitz concludes by reminding us that "we all have the same decision when we stray from Christ and the Church; the decision of whether or not we will 'come to our senses (ourselves),' seek our true identity, turn our backs on false ones, and return to the Father's house, our true home."[156]

The key moment in the Parable of the Prodigal Son is when the son recognizes his true identity — that he is the child of a loving father who is abundantly generous. The same is true for us. No matter how difficult life seems, no matter how great our struggles, no matter how painful our circumstances or afflictions, no matter how confused we are about our own identity, we remain sons and daughters of a loving God who is abundantly generous. And the reassurance of the parable is that no matter how far we fall, God continues to love us and call us back until we reclaim our identity.

Importantly, the prodigal son had to overcome his confusion about who he believed himself to be. He could have fixated on his

---

[156] Ibid., 82.

perception that he was the "bad" son, the "son who turned his back on his father," or the "son who was attracted to debauchery." But none of these labels would have been accurate, since our identity is not measured by our actions or even our attractions.

If you or someone you know is struggling with their identity, or especially with gender dysphoria, recall that each one of us is foremost God's daughter or son. Being His child *is* our identity. What's more, because we are His children, we find all our validation and worth in Him. And that's not all. God loves us so much that he sent His only Son as an eternal offering for our sins so that each of us would have the chance to spend eternity with Him, living in Him.

A damaged family, horrible life choices and experiences, an unusual sexual attraction, or a sense of gender that does not align with our sex — none of these define who we are. At World Youth Day in 2002, Pope St. John Paul II described it this way: "We are not the sum of our weaknesses and failures; we are the sum of the Father's love for us and our real capacity to become the image of His Son."[157] And that makes all the difference.

With all this as background, it is now easier to see the difference between the Church's understanding of our human "identity" and the understanding of our modern, secular culture. While culture sees an infinite range of identities, each subjectively defined and chosen by the individual, the Church sees a son or daughter of God defined by our Creator, independent of our subjective beliefs. While culture says that dignity depends on social recognition and the validation of others, the Church recognizes that our dignity comes from being loved by God and being created in His image and likeness. While culture says that our bodies have no intrinsic meaning, that the sexual act is merely one of pleasure or pain, and that our destiny is to

---

[157] Pope St. John Paul II, "Homily for the Seventeenth World Youth Day" (Toronto, July 28, 2002), no. 5.

have fun while we are alive, the Church acknowledges that we are embodied souls, that the sexual act is designed to express self-giving love and the co-creation of children, and that our destiny is to live eternally with God in Heaven. The difference in the culture's understanding and the Church's understanding of our "identity" is stark indeed. And only the Church's understanding reflects true love of each individual person.

This difference matters in how we live our lives. According to culture, life is a journey in which each person gets to discover himself or herself. In contrast, the Christian journey of discovering self requires detachment, looking at ourselves as God has made us rather than how we might like to be. Clinging and living according to our own sense of self — rather than acknowledging our true identity in God and living according to His instruction book — leads to sin.

We'll conclude with a statement by the Catholic Church's Congregation for the Doctrine of the Faith in its letter to bishops regarding the pastoral care of those with same-sex attractions. This beautiful, loving statement applies equally not only to a sense that one's gender is different than one's sex but to *any* identity that takes our focus off the reality that we are God's children:

> The human person, made in the image and likeness of God, can hardly be adequately described by a reductionist reference to his or her sexual orientation.... The Church provides a badly needed context for the care of the human person when she refuses to consider the person as a "heterosexual" or a "homosexual" and insists that every person has a fundamental Identity: the creature of God, and by grace, his child and heir to eternal life.[158]

---

[158] Congregation for the Doctrine of the Faith, *Letter to the Bishops of the Catholic Church on the Pastoral Care of Homosexual Persons* (October 1, 1986), no. 16.

Indeed. But what happens when we allow someone we love to assert that his or her identity contradicts the clear witness of the body? If that's what they truly feel, is there really any harm in affirming who they believe they are? The answer is yes, and that is the subject of our next chapter.

CHAPTER 6

The Dangers for Those Who
Reject Their Sex

♀ ♂

IF OUR IDENTITY IS as a son or daughter of God, made in His image and likeness, then it stands to reason that if we reject the body God created for us and try to modify or change it, negative consequences and outcomes will flow from that choice. As it turns out, that logic is devastatingly accurate. What is more, it is true not just in the context of gender ideology but in any situation where our own sense of self does not comport with reality.

Consider that it is standard medical and psychological practice to encourage a child with a persistent, mistaken belief that is inconsistent with reality — such as anorexia — to align their belief with reality, not the other way around. Until very recently, this is also how doctors and psychiatrists treated gender-dysphoric children. This approach is consistent with the reality that approximately *eighty to ninety-five percent of children* who experience gender dysphoria will reconcile their "gender identity" with their biological sex if there is no intervention to support or reinforce their dysphoria.[159]

Policies and protocols that treat children who experience gender-atypical thoughts or behaviors as if they *were* the opposite sex interfere with the natural progress of psychosexual development. Such treatments — including affirmation, positive attention, hormone blockers, and surgeries — encourage a child to adhere to his or her false belief that he or she *is* the opposite sex. It would be like affirming people suffering from anorexia that they need to lose weight, encouraging them to eat less — and prescribing liposuction. There is no love in such affirmation.

Again, there are no controlled long-term studies that demonstrate the safety or efficacy of gender-affirming policies and treatments for gender dysphoria in the long term. Not one. And the best long-term study shows that once initial happiness wears off, gender-dysphoric individuals who undergo a surgical transition have *higher* rates of suicide death and psychiatric hospitalization than those who do not.[160] The "truth" of gender ideology — rather than the truth that the Church teaches about our human bodies — is incredibly harmful to those who identify as transgender.

The risks of medical gender affirmation are becoming more apparent

As discussed in greater detail below, there is a global shift *away* from using gender affirmation — using a different name and pronouns, encouraging children to use the opposite sex's privacy facilities or

---

[159] Madeleine S. C. Wallien and Peggy T. Cohen-Kettenis, "Psychosexual Outcome of Gender-Dysphoric Children," *Journal of the American Academy of Child and Adolescent Psychiatry* 47, no. 12 (December 2008): 1413–1423.

[160] See pages 96-97 and note 202; Annette Kuhn et al., "Quality of Life 15 Years After Sex Reassignment Surgery for Transsexualism," *Fertility and Sterility* 92, no. 5 (November 2009): 1685–1689.

sports teams, and the like — as the first-line response to gender-dysphoric youth. That is because gender affirmation is medically dangerous — and not loving.

First, there is no consensus supporting a course of treatment that blocks the onset of puberty for gender-dysphoric youth. Instead, "almost all clinics and professional associations in the world use what's called the *watchful waiting* approach to helping gender diverse (GD) children."[161] Even the American Psychological Association Handbook on Sexuality and Psychology cautions against a rush to affirm that "runs the risk of neglecting individual problems the child might be experiencing and may involve an early gender role transition that might be challenging to reverse if cross-gender feelings do not persist."[162]

What's more, there are obvious risks to gender affirmation in adolescents, particularly when cross-sex hormone treatment suppresses the normal development of secondary sex characteristics and fosters the development of secondary opposite-sex characteristics.

For example, in females, the course of cross-sex hormones (i.e., injecting a woman with high doses of the male hormone testosterone) atrophies and chemically degrades the female sex organs, leading to sexual dysfunction and eventual sterility.[163] That means a girl who begins taking cross-sex hormones may never conceive children — and certainly she will be unable to do so if she continues that

---

[161] James M. Cantor, "Transgender and Gender Diverse Children and Adolescents: Fact-Checking of AAP Policy," *Journal of Sex and Marital Therapy* 46, no. 4 (2020): 307–313.

[162] Walter Bockting, "Transgender Identity Development," chap. 24 in *American Psychological Association Handbook of Sexuality and Psychology*, eds. Deborah L. Tolman and Lisa M. Diamond, vol. 1 (2014), 750.

[163] Michael K. Laidlaw, "The Gender Identity Phantom," *MercatorNet*, November 11, 2018, https://mercatornet.com/the-gender-identity-phantom/23780/. https://perma.cc/N6EW-TGQP

course of treatment for years, as would be necessary to produce some of the secondary sex characteristics of a male.

In addition, females "taking testosterone have shown up to a nearly five-fold increased risk of myocardial infarction," a lack of blood flow to the heart that may also lead to polycythemia (an excess of red blood cells in the body that causes blood to be thicker), which increases the risk of other health issues, including blood clots. These conditions are associated with "a significantly increased risk of cardiovascular disease, coronary heart disease, and death due to both" for younger females.[164]

Some may say that doctors already use puberty blockers to treat children with so-called "precocious puberty" (a developmental condition in which a child's body begins going through puberty before age eight in girls and age nine in boys), so why object to their use to affirm perceived gender? Among other reasons, they are medically different treatments. Treating precocious puberty is a matter of *healing* the body by restoring the body's normal functioning. It involves blocking abnormally early pubertal development but allows puberty to resume at a more typical age, say eleven years old. Puberty then continues through its normal stages until the person reaches full adult sexual maturity. In contrast, using puberty blockers to affirm a perceived "gender identity" involves blocking puberty in children at an age *when puberty normally begins* in order to suppress the ordinary "development of undesired secondary sex characteristics."[165]

---

[164] Michael K. Laidlaw et al., letter to the editor, "Erythrocytosis in a Large Cohort of Transgender Men Using Testosterone: A Long-Term Follow-Up Study on Prevalence, Determinants, and Exposure Years," *Journal of Clinical Endocrinology and Metabolism* 106, no. 12 (December 2021): e5275–e5276.

[165] Johanna Olson-Kennedy et al., "Impact of Early Medical Treatment for Transgender Youth: Protocol for the Longitudinal, Observational Trans Youth Care Study," *JMIR Research Protocols* 8, no. 7 (July 2019).

The difference between the two uses of puberty blockers is highly significant, because in the first instance, delaying puberty does not damage the testes or ovaries. However, blocking puberty to prevent ordinary development maintains a state of immaturity of the testes and ovaries so that even as the child grows in stature, these sexual organs and all the pelvic genitalia remain artificially stunted.[166] Later dosing with "cross-sex hormones (testosterone for girls, estrogen for boys) will not change this condition. As a result, the patient will be infertile as an adult."[167] For the same reason, the child will grow up and be unable to experience satisfaction from sexual intimacy, if sex is possible at all.

Sadly, these medical facts, as well as the extremely weak scientific evidence supporting gender affirmation, have long been known. One report assessing over one hundred follow-up studies on post-operative transsexuals revealed that none proved that sex reassignment is beneficial for patients; in other words, a surgery to purportedly change one's sex did not, over the longer term, meaningfully improve mental health outcomes.[168] And the concerns persist: in a very recent, short-term study, researchers "found no evidence of change in psychological function with GnRHa [puberty blockade] treatment as indicated by parent report (CBCL) or self-report (YSR) of overall problems, internalizing or externalizing problems or self-harm."[169]

---

[166] Michael Laidlaw, Michelle Cretella, and Kevin Donovan, "The Right to Best Care for Children Does Not Include the Right to Medical Transition," *American Journal of Bioethics* 19, no. 2 (February 2019): 75–77.

[167] Ibid.

[168] David Batty, "Mistaken Identity," *The Guardian*, July 30, 2004, https://www.theguardian.com/society/2004/jul/31/health.socialcare. https://perma.cc/7967-6ZCE

[169] Polly Carmichael, et al., "Short-Term Outcomes of Pubertal Suppression in a Selected Cohort of 12 to 15 Year Old Young People with Persistent Gender Dysphoria in the UK," *PLOS One*, February 2, 2021, https://doi.org/10.1371/journal.pone.0243894. https://perma.cc/66JB-YDFT

The harms do not stop there. Girls in the United States may legally obtain a mastectomy at age sixteen, and this procedure carries with it its own unique set of future problems, not least because it is irreversible. Should a girl later change her mind, no future procedure can replace functioning mammary glands, so lactation and breast-feeding are rendered impossible.[170] The psychological effects of such surgery are no less profound. Encouraging medical affirmation is not willing the good of the other.

Even gender affirmation policies can have dangerous, unintended consequences

Policies and protocols that treat children who experience gender-atypical thoughts or behaviors as if they are the opposite sex also interfere with the natural progress of psychosexual development. Such policies encourage a gender-dysphoric youth to adhere to his or her false beliefs and, indeed, help the child to maintain his or her dysphoria — though purportedly with less distress by obligating others in the child's life to go along with it.

The word "purportedly" is important because again: there are no long-term, longitudinal, controlled studies (the gold standard in medicine) that demonstrate the longer term safety or efficacy of gender-affirming policies and treatment for gender dysphoria.[171]

---

[170] Lauren Schmidt, "Psychological Outcomes and Reproductive Issues Among Gender Dysphoric Individuals," *Endocrinology and Metabolism Clinics of North America* 44, no. 4 (December 2015): 773–785, in Michael K. Laidlaw et al., letter to the editor, "Erythrocytosis in a Large Cohort of Transgender Men Using Testosterone."

[171] Cretella, "Gender Dysphoria in Children," 52; E. Abbruzzese, Stephen B. Levine, and Julia W. Mason, "The Myth of 'Reliable Research' in Pediatric Gender Medicine: A Critical Evaluation of the Dutch Studies — and Research That Has Followed," *Journal of Sex and Marital Therapy* (January 2023). This latter source concludes that none of the available research is suitable for making policy or treatment decisions about gender-dysphoric youth.

This lack of studies is especially alarming as treatment moves from social and verbal affirmation to intrusive medical intervention.[172] As one trio of experts observed, children's "gender identity" can fluctuate and change, but if gender-affirming care causes "children to *persist* with their identification as the opposite sex, then many children who would otherwise not need ongoing medical treatment would be exposed to hormonal and surgical interventions."[173]

What's more, it is well recognized that repetition has some effect on the structure and function of a person's brain. This phenomenon, known as "neuroplasticity," means that a child who is encouraged to impersonate the opposite sex may be less likely to reverse course later in life. One study showed that the white matter microstructure of specific brain areas in female-to-male transsexuals was more similar to that of heterosexual males than to that of heterosexual females.[174] Neuroplasticity provides one explanation for the results of that study. This result does not mean that the study subjects had "male" brains from the start; it means that socialization can cause a female brain to begin rewiring itself to look more like a male brain if improperly treated as such. (As noted in chapter four, we know this because "infants' brains are imprinted prenatally by their own endogenous sex hormones" beginning at eight weeks gestation.[175] In other words, male bodies create male brains, and female bodies create female brains. The whole notion "of an 'innate gender fluidity' arising from prenatally 'feminized' or 'masculinized' brains trapped in the wrong body is an ideological belief that has no basis in rigorous science."[176])

---

[172] See page six in Paul Hruz, Lawrence S. Mayer, and Paul R. McHugh, "Growing Pains: Problems with Puberty Suppression in Treating Gender Dysphoria," *The New Atlantis* 52 (Spring 2017): 3–36.

[173] Ibid.; emphasis added.

[174] Rametti et al., "White Matter Microstructure," 199–204.

[175] Cretella, "Gender Dysphoria in Children," 51.

[176] Ibid.

For instance, if a boy repeatedly behaves as a girl, his brain is likely to develop so that eventual, natural realignment with his biological sex is less likely to occur.[177] Under this logic, then, some number of gender-dysphoric children who would naturally come to accept their sex are *prevented* from doing so when gender-affirming policies are imposed on them by adults or encouraged by parents who have bought into gender-identity ideology. The end result is the exact opposite of love — a lifetime of dysphoria and recommended medical treatments that do more harm than good.

In addition, recent research calls into serious question the efficacy of social affirmation. Some researchers had concluded that children who identify as transgender and have strong parental support (but the wrong kind of support, the kind that bolsters the child's confusion rather than the truth of his or her identity) had, at worst, no differences in self-worth or depression compared to control groups, and only slightly higher levels of anxiety. But "a reanalysis of their findings suggests otherwise, with slightly higher levels of depression but significantly and substantively meaningful differences in anxiety and self-worth, and with results favoring [children identifying with their sex], *even when the transgender children had high levels of parental support for their gender transitioning.*"[178] In other words, scientific study shows that true love for a child who identifies as transgender requires us to reject affirmation of that mistaken identity.

---

[177] Ibid., 53.

[178] Walter R. Schumm and Duane W. Crawford, "Is Research on Transgender Children What It Seems? Comments on Recent Research on Transgender Children with High Levels of Parental Support," *The Linacre Quarterly* 87, no. 1 (February 2020): 9–24; emphasis added. In this article, the authors reevaluate data collected in: Kristina R. Olson et al., "Mental Health of Transgender Children Who Are Supported in Their Identities," *Pediatrics* 137, no. 3 (March 2016): e20153223; and Lily Durwood, Katie A. McLaughlin, and Kristina R. Olson, "Mental Health and Self-Worth in Socially Transitioned Transgender Youth," *Journal of the American Academy of Child and Adolescent Psychiatry* 56, no. 2 (February 2017): 116–123.

Importantly, policies that compel social affirmation of gender-dysphoric children within school create confusion for the student announcing a "gender identity" and confusion for other students as well. In addition, such policies do not exist in an ideological vacuum but are typically nested within a larger ideology about how to treat dysphoric children. School-administered gender-affirming actions do not themselves require pharmaceutical or surgical interventions, but puberty suppression, hormone therapy, and surgical interventions are almost invariably in the picture once names, pronouns, and privacy spaces are affirmed.

For schools to adopt such gender-affirmation policies is not only novel, it is a dangerous experiment with no scientific basis to support it; it is an experiment that transforms schoolteachers and administrators into untrained doctors. Gender-affirmation policies amount to bad medicine based on ideology rather than good medicine grounded in sound, scientific evidence and prudential judgment. And bad medicine — just like bad ideas — harms children.

The more that gender-identity ideology is promoted to children, the more children can be expected to become confused about sexuality and to suffer from drastic, unnecessary medical courses that they would not have otherwise chosen. Confusing children is not loving.

Alternatives to gender affirmation

In standard medical and psychological practice, a youth or young adult who has a persistent, mistaken belief that is inconsistent with reality is *not* encouraged to try to align reality — such as their body — with his or her belief.[179] The teenager with anorexia nervosa persistently believes that she is overweight even though her body is not overweight or might even be underweight. No one would suggest that she eat less to align her body with her belief. A boy with body dysmorphic disorder

---

[179] Cretella, "Gender Dysphoria in Children," 51.

persistently believes he is ugly. No one would encourage him to damage or harm his body to match that feeling. Someone with body integrity identity disorder self-identifies as disabled and feels trapped in a fully functioning body, such that they may seek surgery to remove healthy body parts or even to sever their spinal cord. No one would encourage them to actually remove their arm or leg or to sever their spine. And for obvious reasons. Encouraging conduct or surgery to "affirm" the dysphoria "will do nothing to address the underlying psychological problem" and is likely to result in serious harm or even death.[180]

Until quite recently, the same considerations that professionals would apply to anorexia, body dysmorphic disorder, or body integrity identity disorder were also applied when treating gender-dysphoric children. Dr. Kenneth Zucker, long acknowledged as one of the foremost authorities on gender dysphoria in children, spent years helping his patients align their subjective "gender identity" with their objective biological sex. He used psychosocial treatments such as talk therapy, family counseling, and the like to treat gender dysphoria, and he did so with much success.[181] And a systematic follow-up study by Dr. Zucker and his colleagues on the children they treated found that gender dysphoria persisted in only three of the twenty-five female patients, about 12 percent of those treated.[182] Although that is admittedly a small sample size, it is a tremendous success given the lifelong physical and mental health problems associated with affirmation and gender transition.

Dr. Zucker's eminently sound practice is anchored in the reality that each child is immutably either male or female and recognizes

---

[180] Ibid.

[181] Ibid., 50; Kenneth J. Zucker et al., "A Developmental, Biopsychosocial Model for the Treatment of Children with Gender Identity Disorder," *Journal of Homosexuality* 59, no. 3 (2012): 369–397.

[182] Kelley D. Drummond et al., "A Follow-Up Study of Girls with Gender Identity Disorder," *Developmental Psychology* 44, no. 1 (January 2008): 34–45.

that gender dysphoria in children is almost always transient: the vast majority of gender-dysphoric youth naturally reconcile their "gender identity" with their biological sex.[183]

Traditional psychosocial treatments for gender dysphoria, such as those used by Dr. Zucker, work with, rather than against, the facts of science and the predictable rhythms of children's psychosexual development. They allow gender-dysphoric children to reconcile their subjective "gender identity" with their objective biological sex without irreversible effects or using harmful medical treatments.

Research sexologist Dr. Debra Soh explains that the therapeutic approach allows the young to explore the parameters of their gender while being open to the potential of growing comfortable in their sex. In this approach, the therapist seeks to understand relevant factors of the youth's development to include adverse childhood experiences, trauma, and other psychopathology, that is, other factors in the patient's life that might be moving the youth to experience gender dysphoria.[184]

The therapeutic counseling approach has empirical support for its effectiveness in resolving gender dysphoria (GD):

> In conclusion, the adolescents included in this review met criteria for GD and initially requested medical interventions to resolve their difficulties. Over the course of the psychological assessment, they came to understand their

---

[183] Peggy T. Cohen-Kettenis, Henriette A. Delemarre-van de Waal, Louis J. G. Gooren, "The Treatment of Adolescent Transsexuals: Changing Insights," *The Journal of Sexual Medicine* 5, no. 8 (August 2008): 1892–1897; 80 to 95 percent aligned with their biological sex.

Devita Singh, Susan J. Bradley, and Kenneth J. Zucker, "A Follow-Up Study of Boys With Gender Identity Disorder," *Frontiers in Psychiatry* 12 (March 29, 2021); 87.8 percent reconciled their gender identity with their sex in this "largest sample to date of boys clinic-referred for gender dysphoria."

Jiska Ristori and Thomas D. Steensma, "Gender Dysphoria in Childhood," *International Review of Psychiatry* 28, no. 1 (2016): 13–20; 61–98 percent of dysphoric children desisted by adulthood.

[184] Debra Soh, *The End of Gender* (New York: Threshold Editions, 2020).

distress and its alleviation (at that particular point in time) differently and eventually chose not to take a medical (hormonal) pathway and/or identified their gender identity as broadly aligned with their biological sex.[185]

Doctors Anna Churcher Clarke and Anastassis Spiliadis take a very open, pragmatic approach to the question, recognizing that there may be a multiplicity of outcomes but also demonstrating that psychology may resolve dysphoria without resort to risky and often irreversible medical treatments. And that is a prudent approach because although some researchers report that they have identified certain factors associated with the persistence of gender dysphoria into adulthood, there is no evidence that shows that clinicians can identify with any certainty the one-in-twenty child for whom gender dysphoria will, to varying degrees, persist.[186]

Because such a large majority of these children will naturally resolve their confusion — and because the rare exceptions cannot initially be identified — proper medical practice calls for a cautious "wait-and-see" approach for all gender-dysphoric children. This approach can be and often is rightly supplemented by family or individual psychotherapy to identify and treat the underlying mental-health issues, which can include autogynephilia (a male's propensity to be sexually aroused by thinking of himself as a female), distress at unwanted same-sex attractions, autism spectrum disorder, sexual and developmental trauma, transgender obsessive-compulsive disorder,

[185] Anna Churcher Clarke and Anastassis Spiliadis, " 'Taking the Lid off the Box': The Value of Extended Clinical Assessment for Adolescents Presenting with Gender Identity Difficulties," *Clinical Child Psychology and Psychiatry* 24, no. 2 (April 2019): 338–353. This article acknowledges that "it is important to hold onto the multiplicity of possible outcomes."

[186] See, e.g., Thomas D. Steensma et al., "Factors Associated with Desistence and Persistence of Childhood Gender Dysphoria: A Quantitative Follow-Up Study," *Journal of the American Academy of Child and Adolescent Psychiatry* 52, no. 6 (June 2013): 582–590.

pornography addiction, and rapid-onset gender dysphoria, which may present as the belief that one belongs to the opposite sex.

When schools and other institutions begin using preferred pronouns and sex-separated facilities to affirm individual student psychological perceptions, some may believe that it is a harmless expedient to help children feel better about themselves during a difficult time. But as we've discussed, doing so is not harmless; and the risk of harm increases tremendously when it paves the way to medical intervention.

The emerging global trend is to abandon the gender-affirmation model that has gained favor in the United States

Turning back to the common-sense approach of watchful waiting and traditional psychology, gender-medicine practitioners around the globe — including from countries that have been at the forefront of developing gender-identity theory, such as the Scandinavian Peninsula (Sweden, Norway, and Finland) and the United Kingdom — are abandoning the gender affirmation model in favor of conventional exploratory psychological approaches like Dr. Zucker's.

Finland in 2020 issued new guidelines calling for psychotherapy — and not puberty blockers and hormones — as the first preferred response for gender-dysphoric review. The Finnish Health Authority engaged in a systematic review of scientific evidence, concluding that scientific data regarding pediatric transition was inconclusive: "research data on the treatment of dysphoria due to gender identity conflicts in minors is limited."[187] Given that Finland

---

[187] Council for Choices in Health Care in Finland (COHERE Finland), "Medical Treatment Methods for Dysphoria Associated with Variations in Gender Identity in Minors — Recommendation," June 16, 2020, https://bit.ly/Cohere_Finland_GDAinMinorsRx. https://perma.cc/6BR6-WVEK

is a worldwide leader in pediatric gender medicine, the Finnish Health Authority's about-face must be taken seriously.

In 2021, Sweden's largest adolescent gender clinic announced that it would no longer prescribe puberty blockers or cross-sex hormones to youth under eighteen years outside clinical trials.[188] Again, the change reflected growing concern over these interventions given the lack of scientific evidence that they do more good than harm.[189]

In the United Kingdom, litigation against the Tavistock gender clinic — the only nationally funded clinic providing gender-transition interventions for children and young people — led an appellate court to observe that such interventions on

> children for gender dysphoria is controversial. Medical opinion is far from unanimous about the wisdom of embarking on [these interventions] before adulthood. The question raises not only clinical medical issues but also moral and ethical issues, all of which are the subject of intense professional and public debate.[190]

Reviewing these developments, Kamran Abbasi, the editor-in-chief of the *British Medical Journal* (*BMJ*), noted that the United States has "moved in the opposite direction." The *BMJ*'s investigation found "that more and more young people [in the United States] are being offered medical and surgical intervention for gender transition, sometimes bypassing any psychological support." And while this practice is "supported by guidance from [American] medical societies and associations, . . . closer inspection

---

188 "Sweden's Karolinska Ends All Use of Puberty Blockers and Cross-Sex Hormones for Minors Outside of Clinical Studies," *Society for Evidence Based Gender Medicine*, May 5, 2021, https://segm.org/Sweden_ends_use_of_Dutch_protocol. https://perma.cc/4HC9-9DJQ

189 Ibid.

190 *Bell v. Tavistock & Portman NHS Found. Trust* (2021) EWCA (Civ) 1363; available at https://www.judiciary.uk/wp-content/uploads/2022/07/Bell-v-Tavistock-judgment-170921.pdf https://perma.cc/6LUC-VXC7

of that guidance finds that the strength of clinical recommendations is not in line with the strength of the evidence."[191] Stated more plainly, the American medical profession's move to affirm and transition those who identify as transgender is not supported by scientific evidence.

This dangerous shift in the United States toward puberty blockers and hormones and away from counseling was dramatically publicized in 2021, when two prominent gender-affirming doctors "blew the whistle" on sloppy gender-affirmation care. Dr. Marci Bowers is a world-renowned surgeon who performed so-called gender-transition surgery (a vaginoplasty, or "penile inversion") on Jazz Jennings, a boy who reportedly identified as a girl at age two (!), was diagnosed with gender dysphoria at age five, and who has now become a transgender reality television star and children's book author; Erica Anderson is a clinical psychologist at the University of California San Francisco's Child and Adolescent Gender Clinic.[192] Both doctors are males who transitioned to female identities; both are board members for the World Professional Association for Transgender Health, and both say that this "new [gender-affirmation] orthodoxy has gone too far," with Dr. Anderson even opining that "many transgender healthcare providers were treating kids recklessly."[193]

Bowers and Anderson recapped the history of treating gender dysphoria, noting that until about ten years ago, "psychologists

---

[191] Kamran Abbasi, "Caring for Young People with Gender Dysphoria," *British Medical Journal* 380 (March 9, 2023): 553.

[192] Abigail Shrier, "Top Trans Doctors Blow the Whistle on 'Sloppy' Care," *The Free Press*, October 4, 2021, https://www.thefp.com/p/top-trans-doctors-blow-the-whistle. https://perma.cc/327Y-BHT3 Dr. Bowers later claimed these "comments were limited to transfeminine persons, not transmasculine, a point not made" in the Shrier article and expressed disappointment with the "tone and intent of the article." See https://marcibowers.com/transfem/dear-colleagues-clients-andfriends/ https://perma.cc/YR3T-CRVA

[193] Ibid.

treated it with 'watchful waiting' — that is, a method of psychotherapy that seeks to understand the source of a child's gender dysphoria, lessen its intensity, and ultimately help a child grow more comfortable in her own body."[194] But watchful waiting was replaced with so-called "affirmative care," by which doctors are instead urged to "corroborate their patients' belief that they are trapped in the wrong body" while families are pressured to help the child transition to the claimed identity — with activists sometimes telling parents that the choice is transition or suicide.[195] Dr. Bowers's retrospective on the young patients treated with gender-affirming surgeries is revealing: "Honestly, I can't sit here and tell you that they have better — or even as good — results."[196] It is unclear why Dr. Bowers performed the surgery on Jazz, a procedure that went terribly wrong: Jazz required three more surgeries over the next year, gained nearly one hundred pounds in less than two years due to a binge-eating disorder, and deferred admission to Harvard for a full year due to depression.

Additional bad publicity about the shift in American medical practice came from inside a U.S. gender center in 2023. Jamie Reed — a self-described "queer woman … politically to the left of Bernie Sanders" and "married to a transman" — worked for four years as a case manager at the Washington University Transgender Center at St. Louis Children's Hospital. Reed's testimony is worth reading in full, but we will highlight a few key points here.[197] As Reed described it:

> The center's working assumption was that the earlier you
> treat kids with gender dysphoria, the more anguish you

194 Ibid.

195 Ibid.

196 Ibid.

197 Jamie Reed, "I Thought I Was Saving Trans Kids. Now I'm Blowing the Whistle," *The Free Press*, February 9, 2023, https://www.thefp.com/p/i-thought-i-was-saving-trans-kids. https://perma.cc/BSS2-JKR8

can prevent later on. This premise was shared by the center's doctors and therapists. Given their expertise, I assumed that abundant evidence backed this consensus.[198]

But this was not so. Reed left the clinic because:

> I could no longer participate in what was happening there. By the time I departed, I was certain that the way the American medical system is treating these patients [with gender dysphoria] is the opposite of the promise we make to "do no harm." Instead, we are permanently harming the vulnerable patients in our care.[199]

Reed describes clusters of girls with many issues — "depression, anxiety, ADHD, eating disorders, obesity,... autism" — being quickly prescribed testosterone with negative consequences. She pushed back against the center's claims that studies "show these kids often wind up functioning psychosocially as well as or better than their peers," noting the lack of reliable studies that actually show this and emphasizing that "the experiences of many of the center's patients prove how false these assertions are."[200]

When even the foremost practitioners of gender affirmation find "reckless" gender-affirmation treatment occurring in the United States and doubt the efficacy of the practice, it is fair to say that conventional psychotherapy and watchful waiting is not only the safe alternative but the preferred approach to invasive chemicals and surgery. Someone who wills the good of a loved one should choose counseling and therapy over affirmation and medical intervention.

---

[198] Ibid.
[199] Ibid.
[200] Ibid.

But won't transgender children commit suicide if we don't affirm them?

One of the biggest lies we are told is that if we do not affirm a child in his or her expression of "gender identity," the child is likely to commit suicide. You have no doubt heard a variation of this on television or read it online: "I would rather have a living son than a dead daughter." But that's not the real choice presented.

To be sure, children who are dealing with gender dysphoria have shocking suicide rates when compared to the general population. That is why they desperately need our love and care, as Church officials have often reiterated. But scientific studies and experience both show that affirmation and permanently damaging a healthy body are harmful, not helpful, solutions. The "most thorough follow-up of sex-reassigned people — extending over thirty years and conducted in Sweden, where the culture is strongly supportive of the transgendered — documents their lifelong mental struggle. Ten to fifteen years after surgical reassignment, the suicide rate of those who had undergone reassignment surgery *rose* to twenty times that of comparable peers."[201]

Some activists dispute that scientific data (though alternative studies suffer from many flaws, including very small sample sizes and self-selected participants). But it was good enough for President Obama's Centers for Medicare and Medicaid Services — which used this same study to highlight the risks of suicide and psychiatric hospitalization following reassignment surgery:

> *The study identified increased mortality and psychiatric hospitalization compared to the matched controls. The mortality*

[201] Ryan T. Anderson, "Sex Reassignment Doesn't Work. Here Is the Evidence," *The Heritage Foundation*, March 9, 2018, https://www.heritage.org/gender/commentary/sex-reassignment-doesnt-work-here-the-evidence; https://perma.cc/9JJP-V45M emphasis added.

was *primarily due to completed suicides* (19.1-fold greater than in control Swedes), but death due to neoplasm and cardiovascular disease was increased 2 to 2.5 times as well. We note, mortality from this patient population did not become apparent until after ten years. *The risk for psychiatric hospitalization was 2.8 times greater than in controls even after adjustment for prior psychiatric disease* (18 percent). The risk for attempted suicide was greater in male-to-female patients regardless of the gender of the control.[202]

In other words, the study concluded that after surgery, individuals had more mental-health problems, more hospitalizations, and more death from suicides.

These are tragic results, often not apparent until considerable time has passed. Most importantly, these outcomes are directly contrary to the story being told and promoted by gender activists to schools and parents everywhere. That is why we should take with a grain of salt social media reports of those who feel "better" or "great" shortly after a so-called reassignment surgery.

In sum, a person's present experience of his or her sexual identity does not change that person's sex. "While biological sex and 'gender' — or the socio-cultural role of sex as well as 'psychological identity' — can be distinguished, they can never be separated."[203] And strong scientific evidence shows that affirming the mistaken belief that a child is a prisoner of the wrong body is not loving but often ultimately harmful to that child and is likely to make his or her mental health worse.

---

[202] Tamara Syrek Jensen et al., "Final Decision Memorandum on Gender Reassignment Surgery for Medicare Beneficiaries with Gender Dysphoria," *The Centers for Medicare and Medicaid Services* (August 30, 2016), available at https://www.cms.gov/medicare-coverage-database/view/ncacal-decision-memo.aspx?proposed=N&NCAId=282. https://perma.cc/6CQ8-MGXE; emphasis added.

[203] Archbishop Listecki, *Catechesis and Policy*, 2.3.

You may be wondering why some of the United States's leading medical associations support affirmation and surgery when scientific studies show that doing so harms children rather than helps them. An article published in the *Wall Street Journal* and written by a pediatrician and a fellow of the Manhattan Institute claims, "A major reason for this is the [political] capture of institutions such as the AAP," the American Academy of Pediatrics.[204] For instance, in 2022, the AAP's flagship journal, *Pediatrics*, published a study by Dr. Jack Turban, purportedly showing that the shocking increase in the number of young people who identify as transgender was *not* the result of social contagion, a documented phenomenon that mostly impacts teenage girls. The article used that conclusion to argue against state laws that prohibit so-called "gender-affirming medical care."[205]

To prove that point, Dr. Turban uses a supplemental questionnaire that sixteen states adopted based on a Youth Risk Behavior Survey developed by the Centers for Disease Control (CDC). The questionnaire asks the survey respondent if they self-identify as transgender, giving four possible answers: yes, no, I don't know, and I don't understand. In tabulating the data, Dr. Turban leaves out everyone who answered "I don't know," even though a greater percentage of respondents chose that option than those who chose "yes," they self-identify as transgender. But those are the children who are most likely to be impacted by the documented social contagion.

[204] Julia Mason and Leor Sapir, "The American Academy of Pediatrics' Dubious Transgender Science," *The Wall Street Journal*, August 17, 2022, https://www.wsj.com/articles/the-american-academy-of-pediatrics-dubious-transgender-science-jack-turban-research-social-contagion-gender-dysphoria-puberty-blockers-uk-11660732791. https://perma.cc/E7MH-84ND

[205] Jack L. Turban, et al., "Sex Assigned at Birth Ratio Among Transgender and Gender Diverse Adolescents in the United States," *Pediatrics* 150, no.3 (September 2022)

The questionnaire also asks respondents what their "sex" is. Dr. Turban assumes that everyone understood this question to refer to "sex assigned at birth" instead of "gender identity," then cites three surveys to support that understanding, two of which provide no support and one only weak support. In fact, the CDC researcher *who designed the questionnaire* has conceded the "uncertainty as to whether transgender students responded to the sex question with their sex or gender identity."[206]

Also concerning, Dr. Turban's claim about the ratio of boys to girls who identify as transgender conflicts starkly with long-term international trends, documented in peer-reviewed research. That research shows a strong predominance of girls over boys so identifying.[207]

And yet the Church is the institution accused of ignoring scientific inquiry and study.[208]

Gender affirmation can result in other medical harms

One final harm of gender affirmation that the entertainment and media industries rarely discuss is the significance of real sexual differences when it comes to ordinary medical treatment:

---

[206] Dr. Michelle M. Johns et al., "Transgender Identity and Experiences of Violence Victimization, Substance Use, Suicide Risk, and Sexual Risk Behaviors Among High School Students – 19 States and Large Urban School Districts, 2017, *CDC Morbidity and Mortality Weekly Report* 68, no. 3 (January 25, 2019): 67–71.

[207] E.g., Dr. Kenneth J. Zucker, "Adolescents with Gender Dysphoria: Reflections on Some Contemporary Clinical and Research Issues, *Archives of Sexual Behavior* 48, no. 7 (October 2019): 1983–1992.

[208] For a more detailed critique, see Leor Sapir, " 'Trust the Experts' Is Not Enough: U.S. Medical Groups Get the Science Wrong on Pediatric 'Gender Affirming' Care," *The Manhattan Institute*, October 17, 2022, https://www.manhattan-institute.org/how-to-respond-to-medical-authorities-claiming-gender-affirming-care-is-safe. https://perma.cc/29AX-Q5VB

It is now commonly accepted that there is a biological basis for sex differences in a number of common conditions, among them heart disease, stroke, arthritis, dementia, colon cancer, and depression. And there's active research into why other conditions — including obesity, bronchitis, asthma, multiple sclerosis, and thyroid disease — occur more frequently in women than men.[209]

That is why medical experts almost universally agree that doctors and hospitals "need to adjust [their] approaches and develop sex-specific interventions and therapies so both men and women benefit."[210]

These differences show up frequently with respect to types and quantities of medication, therapy regimes, and other treatments. But they can also manifest themselves in important ways in emergency situations. Consider a *New England Journal of Medicine* report about a "man" who "gave birth to a stillborn baby."[211]

The explanation is that the patient was a biological female who had undergone hormonal treatment and had had a double mastectomy and presented to the doctors as a man. The patient's "electronic medical record listed him as a male," and while the patient "was rotund, the nurse chalked that up to obesity." As a result, the patient's "case was not given a high priority," and "several hours passed before doctors" began treatment. Unable to acknowledge the easily preventable harm caused by gender ideology, the *New England Journal* article's lead author wrote, "He was rightly

---

[209] "Medicine Looking Deeper Into Vital Differences Between Women and Men," *Atrium Health Wake Forest Baptist,* https://www.wakehealth.edu/Stories/Differences-Between-Men-and-Women. https://perma.cc/47QR-6PW4

[210] Ibid.

[211] Denise Shick, "Baby Dies Because Doctors Were Told His Pregnant Mother Was A Man," *The Federalist,* May 23, 2019, https://thefederalist.com/2019/05/23/baby-died-doctors-told-mother-man/. https://perma.cc/XW8N-GJMZ

classified as a man.... But that classification threw us off from considering his actual medical needs."[212]

But the patient was not "rightly classified as a man." The problem is that the hospital was too eager to do what the patient and culture demanded: to accept the patient's self-professed identity rather than the patient's sex. Had the hospital classified the patient by sex—female—the course of treatment likely would have been different and more effective. In the end, the failure to treat this woman properly ended in the death of an innocent: had she been treated as a woman and not as a man, "the baby might have lived."[213]

The tragedy of this lost baby is a perfect example of the harms that follow when we refuse to love by affirming God's truth — and nature's reality. Regrettably, there are many others, some of which will be discussed in the next chapter.

[212] Ibid.
[213] Ibid.

CHAPTER 7

Detransitioners

♀ ♂

WE ARE CALLED TO journey *with* those who struggle to follow God's plan for their life. In fact, the Church instructs us "to treat persons with same-sex attraction and gender dysphoria with dignity and respect"; "all unjust discrimination is to be avoided."[214] That is why many Catholic parishes host "Courage" chapters to walk alongside those with same-sex attractions and help them understand and follow the Church's teachings about human sexuality. Yet we are often reluctant to speak up when it comes to gender identity, even as the movement to identify as transgender becomes an epidemic, especially for young girls.[215]

---

[214] Bishop John F. Doerfler, *Created in the Image and Likeness of God: An Instruction on Some Aspects of the Pastoral Care of Persons with Same-Sex Attraction and Gender Dysphoria,* July 29, 2021, 6; available at https://dioceseofmarquette.org/pastoral-messages-instructions-and-resources. https://perma.cc/F5U7-PYQZ

[215] Abigail Shrier, *Irreversible Damage: The Transgender Craze Seducing Our Daughters* (Washington, DC: Regnery Publishing, 2020).

In a culture that is quick to affirm and offer adulation to children who identify as transgender, it is important that families be fully informed about what it means to purportedly "change one's sex." And that requires us to know — and truly understand — the stories of detransitioners, those who took steps, social or medical or both, to present as a member of the opposite sex and then sought once again to present as their actual, biological sex.

A recent survey of detransitioners revealed that more than half felt they had been given insufficient information before making the profound medical decision to transition.[216] And there are now strong, though generally unreported, trends *away* from using gender-affirming policies, precisely because of the concern that such policies tend to harm, rather than help, gender-dysphoric children. A few personal stories from these detransitioners drive home the importance of loving those who struggle by speaking the truth with charity rather than simply giving in to whatever they seem to believe they want.

Walt

When Walt Heyer was four years old, his grandmother repeatedly — and over a number of years — cross-dressed him in a purple dress she made just for him and told Walt how pretty he was "as a girl." Eventually, Walt's parents discovered this and cut off his unsupervised visits with his grandmother. But a teenage uncle caught wind of what had happened and targeted Walt with taunting, which was followed by sexual abuse before he was ten years old.[217]

[216] Becky McCall, "Transgender Regret: Detransitioners Got Poor Care When Transitioning," *Medscape Medical News*, November 4, 2021, www.medscape.com/viewarticle/962270. https://perma.cc/AKU2-AV5C

[217] Walt Heyer, "Hormones, Surgery, Regret: I Was a Transgender Woman for 8 Years — Time I Can't Get Back," *USA Today*, February 11, 2019, usatoday.com/story/opinion/voices/2019/02/11/transgender-debate-transitioning-sex-gender-column/1894076002/. https://perma.cc/4DRC-XZ5B

As a result of the abuse, Walt no longer wanted to be a boy. Cross-dressing was his escape. At night, he begged God to change him into a girl, thinking that this would make the adults in his life affirm and accept him. He would be "safe." Walt continued cross-dressing into adulthood, until he turned forty. Although married and a father, he felt torn apart by his desire to be female.[218]

Walt found one of the nation's leading gender specialists, Dr. Paul Walker, who diagnosed Walt with gender identity disorder, what the American Psychological Association now calls gender dysphoria. Dr. Walker told Walt that his childhood trauma was not the cause of his current gender distress and opined that cross-sex hormones and sex-change surgery "was the only solution." Walt followed Dr. Walker's advice and at age forty-two underwent genital reconfiguration and received breast implants and other "feminizing procedures." He officially changed his name to "Laura," and his childhood dream of living as a woman began.[219]

At first, his transformation seemed to be a success. Walt felt that he had a "fresh start" and "was giddy with excitement." But then reality hit. Walt's former wife and children were devastated. And, as he describes it, "hidden underneath the makeup and female clothing was the little boy hurt by childhood trauma." In fact, Walt was again feeling gender-dysphoric, but now "felt like a male inside a body refashioned to look like a woman." He was suicidal.[220]

Despite living as a woman for eight years, Walt had many questions: "Why hadn't the recommended hormones and surgery worked? Why was I still distressed about my gender identity? Why wasn't I happy being Laura? Why did I have strong desires to be Walt again?" And so he bravely pursued help from a psychologist to deal

[218] Ibid.
[219] Ibid.
[220] Ibid.

with the trauma he had suffered as a child. He knew "it was the only way to address the underlying conditions driving" his continued feelings of gender dysphoria.[221]

By the age of fifty-five, Walt had changed his legal name back and undid — to the extent possible — the surgeries. But there is permanent damage to his body, and he requires an ongoing hormone regimen. Walt is confident that if he had not been misled by medical practitioners and media stories, he would not have made the choices that caused him to suffer the way he did. And he now understands the truth: "Hormones and surgery may alter appearances, but nothing changes the immutable fact of your sex."[222]

To his great credit, Walt now ministers to others who want to take back their lives after a sex transition using his popular website, sexchangeregret.com. He says that "hundreds of transgender-identifying people have asked for [his] help."[223] And Walt has written a book, *Trans Life Survivors*, with stories of regret and detransitioning as told by thirty individuals who have experienced it.

Benji

Benji's story is told in Abigail Shrier's book *Irreversible Damage: The Transgender Craze Seducing Our Daughters*. In this groundbreaking book, Ms. Shrier, a *Wall Street Journal* writer, dug into the epidemic of large groups of female students — from middle school to college — suddenly coming out together as "transgender." She offered parents advice about how to protect their daughters from falling into a transgender social contagion.

[221] Ibid.
[222] Ibid.
[223] Aliya Kuykendall, "Detransitioned Man Answers Questions About Transgenderism," *The Stream*, May 7, 2019, stream.org/detransitioned-man-answers-questions-about-transgenderism/. https://perma.cc/QKQ9-MUDL

Chapter ten of her book introduces the reader to Benji, a Canadian woman. A skilled musician on violin, viola, harp, and piano, as well as a voracious reader, Benji became uncomfortable and self-conscious when she began developing breasts at only nine years old. She suffered from anorexia, depression, and physical abuse, and she started smoking marijuana and engaging in other dangerous behavior.[224]

At age thirteen, Benji ran across Tumblr and YouTube videos of females raving about their transition to become men. Shrier relates what happened next: "Feeling unfeminine, awkward in her body, and unhappy at home, Benji found the possibility of escape enrapturing. She never doubted the accuracy of the purely positive accounts of medical transition" that she had viewed online. She "decided privately that her story matched the video accounts of trans men online. She was trans too." And so Benji announced she was trans on a Tumblr account and received an outpouring of support from total strangers.[225]

Benji's online friends were "unconditionally supportive, showering her with praise." But then adults — primarily men who identified as women — began asking Benji to "sext." At age fourteen, "she was too curious and far too agreeable not to comply." And even when she tried to say no, these adults accused her of "making them feel bad about their sexual predilections" and accused her "of transphobic oppression."[226]

When Benji got to high school, she joined the Gay-Straight Alliance, changed her pronouns at school, and gave up her old name, Eva, for Benji, without letting her parents in on her double life. Then, after police responded to a domestic dispute at her home, a social worker arranged for Benji to see a therapist. Benji disclosed her secret. The therapist declared that Benji was "definitely trans," though with hindsight, Benji now thinks the therapist was biased.[227]

---

[224] Shrier, *Irreversible Damage*, 185–86.
[225] Ibid., 186.
[226] Ibid., 187.
[227] Ibid.

Benji began wearing a breast binder, a device that compresses breast tissue to give someone the appearance of having a flat chest. Benji also began cutting her hair short and wearing men's clothes exclusively. She became more involved in local LGBTQ youth groups, inhabiting a gender-ideology world that she now characterizes as a "cult" that "brainwashed" her. She continued to have problems with her parents, and, when she complained about them online, LGBTQ adults started to give her advice about how to run away. As Benji now sees it, these adults were "weaponizing it against me to kind of draw me into their community and draw me away from anyone who would give me rational ways of thinking about my life." She started to believe that trans-identified people were the only ones she could trust.[228]

As Benji sank further into depression and gender dysphoria, she "came to equate cross-sex hormones and gender surgery with salvation, the necessary precondition of a happy life." She was afraid that taking testosterone might adversely impact some of her preexisting health problems. But "questioning the panacea of medical transition was strictly verboten" in the LGBTQ community. When Benji "followed" a gay man on social media who did not buy gender ideology, one of Benji's queer friends circulated a screenshot and implored their mutual friends to "cancel" and block Benji. Benji confronted the friend, who told her she should not talk to such people: "You will lose your identity, you will stop being trans. You will literally die if you talk to these people."[229]

Benji finally reached a turning point after talking to a friend who was undergoing chemotherapy treatment and asked Benji why she would undergo surgery "when you're not literally going to die from having breasts." Benji stopped communicating with the gender activists and acknowledged she was a woman, though she decided to keep

---

[228] Ibid., 187–188.
[229] Ibid., 189–191.

the name Benji. Reflecting on her experience and reading more about the issue, Benji has become more convinced that the medical system and mental health professionals are hurting trans-identified teens rather than helping them. Her public comments to that effect have resulted in repeated social-media cancellations.[230]

Carol

Carol is a detransitioner from California whose story "has lessons for trans medicine," per *The Economist*.[231] As a self-described "butch" female, Carol "was routinely treated with slight contempt" and thought life "would be easier if she were a man." After taking testosterone and undergoing a double mastectomy, the world seemed to be a much friendlier place.[232]

That feeling changed all too soon. After two years of injecting testosterone, Carol "began to suffer awful side effects." These effects included "extremely painful" atrophy of her vagina and uterus, increased cholesterol, palpitations, and anxiety-induced panic attacks. After going on antidepressants, Carol had a "light-bulb moment." With the help of the antidepressants, she realized that she did not have to transition and that her feelings of being in the wrong body did not actually make her a male.[233]

Carol came to realize that her gender dysphoria was rooted in a family upbringing that imposed "rigid gender roles" in which women were understood to be "less than men." By her early twenties, she wanted to transition but "was told she had to live as a man for six months before being approved for treatment, and the thought of

---

[230] Ibid., 191–193.
[231] "Portrait of a Detransitioner as a Young Woman," *The Economist*, November 6, 2021, https://economist.com/united-states/2021/11/06/portrait-of-a-detransitioner-as-a-young-woman. https://perma.cc/KEP3-KJK9
[232] Ibid.
[233] Ibid.

using the men's toilet was intolerable." By Carol's mid-thirties, she could get a testosterone prescription without a therapist; in thirty-five states, including California, Planned Parenthood follows an "informed consent" model, which means that patients who identify as trans do not need a note from a therapist. But Carol desired to "do it right" and saw a therapist anyway. Unfortunately, the therapist almost immediately recommended testosterone instead of resolving underlying mental health issues due to Carol's childhood trauma. Within months, Carol underwent a double mastectomy.[234]

After four years of living as a man, Carol detransitioned. Her experience vividly shows the dangers of a gender-affirming standard of care in the United States, one that simply accepts self-diagnosis rather than truly investigating why a patient is experiencing gender incongruence. Indeed, a survey by Dr. Lisa Littman of one hundred detransitioners found that a "majority (55 percent) felt that they did not receive an adequate evaluation from a doctor or mental health professional before starting transition." Sixty percent of those surveyed detransitioned after growing more comfortable identifying with their sex, and 38 percent concluded that their dysphoria was caused by abuse, trauma, or a mental health issue.[235]

As for Carol, "detransitioning was the hardest thing she has done." While her cholesterol levels went back to normal within months, "she still has some facial hair and a deep voice," and her mastectomy "is like any loss: it dissipates but it never completely goes away." So she now devotes "a lot of time campaigning for other detransitioners' stories to be heard," which "is not easy work" since

---

[234] Ibid.

[235] Lisa Littman, "Individuals Treated for Gender Dysphoria with Medical and/or Surgical Transition Who Subsequently Detransitioned: A Survey of 100 Detransitioners," *Archives of Sexual Behavior* 50, no. 8 (November 2021): 3353-3369.

"outspoken detransitioners are often maligned."[236] Indeed, Dr. Littman's study revealed that "only 24 percent of respondents informed their clinicians that they had detransitioned."[237] That means 76 percent of the detransitioners *never said anything to their doctors at all* despite reversing their transitions — leaving the doctors with the misimpression that all was well with their former clients.

James

In 2015, James Shupe penned an article in the *New York Times* about his decision to live as a woman, declaring his desire to live "authentically as the woman that I have always been" while "trad[ing] my white male privilege to become one of America's most hated minorities."[238] Then, in 2016, James decided he was not a woman or a man but nonbinary, and he sued and persuaded an Oregon judge to allow him to identify as neither male nor female but as a third sex. But in 2019, he decided "to live again as the man that I am."[239]

James's story began when, after convincing himself he was a woman while suffering a mental-health crisis, he "visited a licensed nurse practitioner in early 2013 and asked for a hormone prescription," threatening, "if you don't give me the drugs, I'll buy them off the internet." Although the nurse had never even met James before, she phoned for a prescription the same day, ignoring his PTSD from eighteen years of military service and possibly other mental-health problems stemming from childhood physical and sexual

[236] "Portrait of a Detransitioner as a Young Woman."

[237] Littman, "Individuals Treated for Gender Dysphoria."

[238] Jamie Shupe, "Transgender Lives: Your Stories," *The New York Times*, https://www.nytimes.com/interactive/2015/opinion/transgender-today/stories/jamie-shupe. https://perma.cc/CNP4-NSUK

[239] James Shupe, "I Was America's First 'Nonbinary' Person. It Was All a Sham," *The Daily Signal*, March 10, 2019, dailysignal.com/2019/03/10/i-was-americas-first-non-binary-person-it-was-all-a-sham/. https://perma.cc/KGV3-J7J3

abuse by an uncle who shared his first name as well as from years of watching pornography.[240]

James continued cross-sex hormones and began therapy at a Pittsburgh gender clinic so that he could get the approvals needed for planned reassignment surgery. Only a single therapist tried to stop him, but after James filed a complaint against her, she backed down; in the medical community, there is little support for those who counsel prudence. And no therapist even discussed with James whether he had stereotypical feelings of females. Instead, his new therapist affirmed his female identity.[241]

"The best thing that could have happened," says James, "would have been for someone to order intensive therapy." Instead, his mental illness was ignored and even treated as wellness, and he found himself "in the women's bathroom with people's wives and daughters." And then, three years into his change from man to woman, "despite having taken or been injected with every hormone and anti-androgen concoction" available, James realized that he "didn't look anything like a female," and that "biological sex is immutable." So he asked two of his doctors to help him become nonbinary, that is, not identifying as a man or woman, and both doctors "readily agreed."[242]

The doctors gave James a copious amount of hormones, "the equivalent of twenty birth control pills per day," and wrote him a sex-change letter. James then went to Oregon state court where he persuaded a state-court judge with a transgender child to declare him "the first legally recognized nonbinary person in the country." Shortly thereafter, with the help of an LGBTQ legal-aid group, James successfully changed his birth certificate to say that his sex was "unknown." (Lambda Legal then used the Oregon court order to persuade a Colorado federal

240 Ibid.
241 Ibid.
242 Ibid.

judge to direct the U.S. State Department to issue a passport with an "X", for nonbinary, to represent the sex of another plaintiff.[243])

Finally, James came to realize that his "sex change to nonbinary was a medical and scientific fraud." And as he began in 2017 to publicly oppose "the sterilization and mutilation of gender-confused children and transgender military service members," the help from LGBTQ organizations dried up, and overnight he went "from being a liberal media darling to a conservative pariah." As James explains it, he did "not have any disorders of sexual development," all his "sexual confusion was in [his] head," and he "should have been treated" with therapy. "Instead," James writes, "at every step, doctors, judges, and advocacy groups indulged my fiction."[244]

In January 2019, James reclaimed his male sex. He explains:

> Two fake gender identities couldn't hide the truth of my biological reality. There is no third gender or third sex. Like me, intersex people are either male or female. Their condition is the result of a disorder of sexual development, and they need help and compassion.[245]

Sadly, human nature being what it is, some people fall back, and in 2022, James issued a statement declaring a female identity once again. But James's story illustrates the impact of transgender ideology on the American legal and medical communities: to accommodate — rather than care for and love fragile individuals — doctors, counselors, and lawyers cause harm to those individuals and those who truly care for and love them. In James's words, his "wife, daughter, and the American taxpayers [who provided and paid for his nonbinary passport and driver's license] are the real victims."[246]

---

[243] Ibid.
[244] Ibid.
[245] Ibid.
[246] Ibid.

Chloe

"After being exposed for hours at a time to online transgender influencers," explains a medical malpractice complaint filed by Chloe Cole against several of her former doctors, Permanente Medical Group, and Kaiser Foundation Hospitals, "Chloe developed the erroneous idea that she was a boy."[247] Things escalated quickly. By age twelve, Chloe decided she was a boy; by age thirteen, Chloe started puberty blockers and testosterone; and by age fifteen, Chloe had undergone a double mastectomy before having a change of heart. Chloe detransitioned when she turned sixteen.[248]

As explained in the lawsuit, Chloe struggled with mental problems, including "body dysmorphia, autism, anxiety, and more."[249] But her doctors and health care institutions "never meaningfully discussed nor attempted to treat with psychotherapy Chloe's struggles and these underlying conflicts."[250] In fact, the complaint alleges, these health care professionals "never told Chloe that puberty changes are a struggle for most people, particularly females, and that negative emotions tend to increase during puberty, and further that it takes time to settle into these changes to one's evolving body."[251] The complaint maintains that Chloe's doctors failed to discuss even basic "components of psychotherapy for young adolescent girls," resulting in a failure to obtain her informed consent.[252]

As the complaint describes the situation, there was very little authentic love demonstrated in this series of catastrophic medical decisions:

---

[247] Chloe E. Brockman a/k/a Chloe Cole v. Kaiser Foundation Hospitals, Inc., a California Corporation et al., San Joaquin County Superior Courts, California, Compl. ¶ 3, available at https://libertycenter.org/wp-content/uploads/2023/02/Complaint1.pdf. https://perma.cc/9XFE-QM3E

[248] "Legal Action May Change Transgender Care in America," *The Economist*, March 7, 2023, https://www.economist.com/united-states/2023/03/07/legal-action-may-change-transgender-care-in-america. https://perma.cc/CKR9-G99W

[249] *Chloe E. Brockman v. Kaiser Foundation Hospitals et al.*, Compl. ¶ 2.

[250] Ibid., ¶ 28.

[251] Ibid.

[252] Ibid., ¶¶ 28, 42-44.

Chloe was the victim of Defendants [her doctors] who did not have any interest in taking the time necessary to sit with her and perform the regular, weekly psychotherapy that Chloe needed. Defendants grossly breached the standard of care by pushing Chloe into this harmful experimental treatment regimen without a proper period of psychological evaluation, without evaluating and treating her serious co-morbidities, without providing informed consent, and while actively utilizing emotionally super-charged and false information to derail the rational decision-making process of Chloe and her parents. Defendants were not "caring" for Chloe, they were experimenting on her, and doing so all to their own great financial benefit.[253]

Today, Chloe publicly advocates for other teenagers experiencing gender dysphoria, encouraging medical and mental health professionals to investigate and treat underlying issues rather than quickly recommending invasive treatments without discussing alternatives.

Tip of the iceberg

Stories like Walt's, Benji's, Carol's, James's, and Chloe's are just the beginning. As noted above, Walt has published a book full of stories by those who have detransitioned.[254] There is a Reddit community of detransitioners with thousands upon thousands of posts and comments.[255] Websites collect stories from detransitioners who want the world to know what happened to them.[256] March 12 has been designated as the

---

[253] Ibid., ¶ 8.

[254] Walt Heyer, *Trans Life Survivors* (self-pub., Bowker Identifier Services, 2018).

[255] "Detransition Subreddit," *Reddit*, Reddit.com/r/detrans/. https://perma.cc/3J5D-ZUPL

[256] See, for example: https://post-trans.com/Detransition-English; and https://detransvoices.com/read-stories/. https://perma.cc/KL6X-PVRN

annual Detransition Awareness Day.[257] And yet activists would prefer that all the detransitioners be silenced.

In early 2021, a *60 Minutes* producer reached out to detransitioners to cover their stories. But by the time the show finally aired, gender activists had pressured CBS and *60 Minutes* to give the bulk of the show's minutes to the activists' propaganda instead, leaving only a few, short minutes for the detransitioners. Groups like GLAAD (Gay & Lesbian Alliance Against Defamation) then vilified the show for giving detransitioners *any* opportunity to tell their stories.[258] GLAAD tweeted that *60 Minutes* had "aired a shameful segment fearmongering about trans youth. Parents of trans youth could walk away with the false belief that young people are being rushed into medical transition. That is simply untrue."[259] But stories such as those of Walt, Benji, Carol, James, Chloe, and countless others show that rush is precisely what is happening. And "while a great number of young people have come forward to say they were deeply harmed, corporations that were once set up to protect LGBTQ youth — like HRC, ACLU, and GLAAD — have done all they can to sweep them under a rug,"[260] hardly willing the good for those who have been harmed.

Detransitioners are not the only group of people being silenced for their objections to gender ideology. Female athletes, teachers, victims of domestic assault, and many others who are being harmed by gender ideology are rarely given a public space to tell *their* stories either. We will discuss some of them in the next chapter.

---

257 "Detransitioners Need to Be Heard," *MercatorNet*, March 9, 2022, https://mercatornet.com/detransitioners-need-to-be-heard/77954/. https://perma.cc/CFM3-NG5M

258 J. D. Robertson, "Detrans Youth Stories They Didn't Want You to Hear, in *60 Minutes* or Less," *The Velvet Chronicle*, May 31, 2021, https://thevelvetchronicle.com/detrans-youth-stories-they-didnt-want-you-to-hear-60-minutes-or-less/. https://perma.cc/45KJ-5DBW

259 Ibid.

260 Ibid.

CHAPTER 8

How Gender Ideology Harms Others

WHEN WE DEVIATE FROM God's plan, we harm not only ourselves but others too. As C. S. Lewis beautifully explains in *Mere Christianity*, our society is like "a fleet of ships sailing in formation."[261] If one ship goes off course, it invariably impacts the others. That is particularly true when our understanding of things as fundamental as gender and sexuality goes astray.

This chapter will explore some of the third-party harms caused by gender ideology.[262] It will start with the story of two high school boys in Connecticut who identified as female and then "won" thirteen state track-and-field championships. The chapter will then review how gender ideology has harmed women and girls in private spaces — such as showers, restrooms, locker rooms, and dormitories — including how

---

[261] C. S. Lewis, "The Three Parts of Morality," bk. 3, ch. 1 of *Mere Christianity* (New York: Touchstone, 1996), 70–71.

[262] Many of the legal cases discussed in this chapter include clients represented by Alliance Defending Freedom, the public-interest law firm for which the author also works as a lawyer.

the City of Anchorage, Alaska, engaged in a battle with a women's shelter that prohibits males-who-identify-as-females from sleeping in the same room as women who have been trafficked and abused.

The chapter will also examine cases of teachers and professors punished for declining to speak lies about human sexuality, as well as medical professionals who have been silenced or fired merely for questioning whether a child's self-professed "gender identity" should be automatically affirmed. The chapter will conclude with a discussion about parents faced with schools that secretly affirm their child's "gender identity" without disclosure, and governments that threaten to remove children from parents who object to gender affirmation and transition.

A note of caution: reading these stories and those in the next chapter may inspire frustration, anger, and a desire for retribution. But that is not our calling. We must identify and resist injustice. We must continually proclaim the truth. And we must do these things in charity, channeling our emotions to transform culture and accompany individuals.

Athletics and other opportunities for women

Highschool track athlete Chelsea Mitchell was the fastest girl in Connecticut in 2019. But the record books don't reflect that fact. Instead, the official records state that she lost four women's state championship track titles, two all-New England awards, and numerous other places on winners' podiums — to male runners who identified and competed as females.[263]

Her story begins with the Connecticut Interscholastic Athletic Conference, which adopted a competition policy that allows students to compete in women's athletics based on their own "gender

---

[263] Chelsea Mitchell, "I Was the Fastest Girl in Connecticut. But Transgender Athletes Made It an Unfair Fight," *Alliance Defending Freedom*, May 26, 2021, https://adflegal.org/article/i-was-fastest-girl-connecticut-transgender-athletes-made-it-unfair-fight. https://perma.cc/6QXX-J328

identification" rather than their sex.[264] So if a boy identifies as a girl, he can compete against girls, although "scientists agree that males and females are materially different with respect to the main physical attributes that contribute to athletic performance."[265] In fact, according to studies (which simply document experience and common sense), "even the best females are not competitive for the win against males."[266]

In 2017, Andraya Yearwood, a biologically male student, identified as female and started competing in women's track and field in Connecticut.[267] As a freshman, Yearwood won two State Class championships and ranked third in the State Open championship.[268]

The following school year, Terry Miller, another biologically male athlete, also identified as female and began competing in girls' track events. Miller previously competed as a male runner and never advanced to a State Class or State Open championship. But in the women's division, Miller was able to take first place at the 2018 State Open championship, and Yearwood finished second. Chelsea Mitchell, who was then a freshman, finished fourth.[269]

The 2019 events ended similarly. In a preliminary State Class competition, Miller and Yearwood finished second and third, bumping freshman Ashley Nicoletti from qualifying for the final State Class race. And in a preliminary State Open championship race, Miller and Yearwood took first and second, which prevented Selina

---

[264] Soule v. Connecticut Association of Schools, Inc., 2nd Circuit Court, No. 21-1365, Appellants' Brief (July 9, 2021); available at https://adflegal.org/sites/default/files/2021-10/Soule-v-Connecticut-Association-of-Schools-Appellate-Opening-Brief-07-09-2021.pdf. https://perma.cc/X6UD-CQ2J

[265] Ibid. (Quoting pages 69 and 92 of Doriane Lambelet Coleman, Michael J. Joyner, and Donna Lopiano, "Re-Affirming the Value of the Sports Exception to Title IX's General Non-Discrimination Rule," *Duke Journal of Gender Law and Policy* 27 (2020): 69–134).

[266] Ibid. (Quoting page 115 of Coleman et al., "Re-Affirming the Value.")

[267] Ibid.

[268] Ibid., 6–7.

[269] Ibid., 7.

Soule from advancing to the final State Open championship race. In the State Open final, Miller and Yearwood again finished first and second. That left Chelsea Mitchell — the fastest female athlete in Connecticut — in third place. And Chelsea and Alanna Smith lost to Miller in yet another State Open championship race the same year.[270]

From 2017 to 2019, biological males Yearwood and Miller "won" *thirteen* women's statechampionship titles, taking more than sixty-eight opportunities from female athletes to advance and participate in high-level women's track competitions. In seven state-level events, Yearwood and Miller prevailed in thirteen out of fourteen women's championships, with a female competitor winning just one.[271]

Chelsea Mitchell, Selina Soule, Ashley Nicoletti, and Alanna Smith had trained intensely for years to shave precious seconds — indeed, fractions of seconds — off their times so they could advance in competitions, win meets and championships, and pursue college scholarships.[272] Yet when these brave young women sued under Title IX — the federal law that ensures a fair playing field for female athletes — a federal judge threw out their case. He ordered the women's lawyer not to refer to Yearwood and Miller as "males" but instead as "transgender females." He said he considered the latter term "more accurate" and "consistent with science"[273] — which is factually incorrect, as discussed in chapter four.

Unfortunately, what happened to Chelsea, Selina, Ashley, and Alanna is just the beginning. A male athlete who used to compete for New Zealand in men's weightlifting now identifies as a woman and took two gold medals and a silver in the women's division at the 2019 Pacific Games.[274] A male cyclist who identifies as a woman took first

---

[270] Ibid., 7–8.

[271] Ibid., 8.

[272] Ibid.

[273] Ibid., 10.

[274] "Weightlifter Hubbard Becomes Lightning Rod for Criticism of Transgender Policy," *Reuters*, July 30, 2019, https://reut.rs/2SVN6nN. https://perma.cc/WXQ3-VK5Z

place in a women's bracket of the 2018 International Masters Track Cycling World Championships.[275] A thirty-five-time winner on the women's national cyclocross circuit announced that she retired from the sport she loves after finishing in fourth place between two men identifying as women. As she said in one interview:

> It has become increasingly discouraging to train as hard as I do only to have to lose to a man with the unfair advantage of an androgenized body that intrinsically gives him an obvious advantage over me, no matter how hard I train.[276]

The stories continue: in 2017, a biological male identifying as a woman defeated a top professional female Mixed Martial Arts fighter, breaking an orbital bone in her skull and causing a concussion. The victim, Tamikka Brents, said that she has "fought a lot of women and have never felt the strength that I felt in a fight as I did that night."[277] No wonder; she was fighting a man.

Some states have acted to protect women from this unfair competition. As of this book's publication, twenty-one states — Alabama, Arizona, Arkansas, Florida, Idaho, Indiana, Iowa, Kansas, Kentucky, Louisiana, Mississippi, Montana, North Dakota, Oklahoma, South Carolina, South Dakota, Tennessee, Texas, Utah, West

---

[275] Kirsten Frattini, "McKinnon is First Transgender Woman to Win World Title," *Cycling News*, October 16, 2018, https://bit.ly/2PPFGQI. https://perma.cc/X3PM-GJ9E

[276] Ryan Gaydos, "US Cyclocross Champion Reveals She Retired from Sport Over Emergence of Transgender Athletes in Women's Sports," *Fox News*, March 23, 2023, https://www.foxnews.com/sports/us-cyclocross-champion-reveals-she-retired-sport-emergence-transgender-athletes-womens-sports. https://perma.cc/CRG4-AH69

[277] Ian Shutts, "After Being TKO'd by Fallon Fox, Tamikka Brents Says Transgender Fighters in MMA 'Just Isn't Fair,' " *LowKickMMA*, April 19, 2017, https://www.lowkickmma.com/after-being-tkod-by-fallon-fox-tamikka-brents-says-transgender-fighters-in-mma-just-isnt-fair/. https://perma.cc/N3RL-PDU5

Virginia, and Wyoming—have all passed similar "Save Women's Sports" bills that require men's and women's athletic teams to regulate participation by sex rather than "gender identity."

Athletic associations are starting to do the same. But progress is slow, and there is still much controversy. For example, the NCAA enacted a policy requiring males competing as females to undergo mandatory testosterone testing, but that policy has since been changed. And in any case, testosterone levels often mean little after a male body has already gone through puberty. Even after two years of female hormone therapy, University of Pennsylvania's Lia Thomas went from being the 462nd-ranked male collegiate swimmer to being a record-setting, first-ranked female swimmer in the 2021–22 collegiate swim season. Sixteen members of the UPenn swim team sent a letter to the university and the Ivy League asking them not to challenge the NCAA's policy (when it was still in effect) at least requiring testosterone testing. While the teammates said they "fully support" Thomas's professed gender identity and transition from male to female, they recognized "that when it comes to sports competition ... the biology of sex is a separate issue from someone's gender identity."[278] This reasoning does not capture the full scope of the issue, but standing up for women's sports in the current cultural climate was certainly courageous.

World Rugby took a much stronger stand, becoming the first international sports federation to declare that "transgender women who transitioned post-puberty and have experienced the biological effects of testosterone during puberty and adolescence *cannot* currently play women's rugby."[279] Why? "From puberty onwards," testosterone in

[278] Jacob Lev, "16 UPenn Swimmers Ask School Not to Challenge Transgender Policy That Could Block Teammate Lia Thomas from Competing," *CNN*, February 4, 2022, https://www.cnn.com/2022/02/04/us/lia-thomas-ncaa-transgender-policy-letter/index.html. https://perma.cc/5N9G-EYBV

[279] "Transgender Women Guidelines," *World Rugby*, https://www.world.rugby/the-game/player-welfare/guidelines/transgender/women, https://perma.cc/TM7J-L8D3 accessed; emphasis added.

males results in physical development — including muscle mass, reduced fat, increased cardiovascular and respiratory function, and longer, denser, larger skeletal systems that can produce more force — that "account for large sporting performance differences between males and females."[280] That is why we rarely see women identifying as men trying — and succeeding — to compete as men. Those differences that World Rugby documented include "gaps between 9 percent and 15 percent for running, swimming and jumping events, between 15 percent and 35 percent for functional tasks like kicking, throwing, bowling and weightlifting, and in excess of 50 percent for tasks that involve upper body force production."[281]

The association was also concerned about injury risk to female athletes from male athletes who identify as females, and it recognized that "the actual testosterone level, measurable in the body, is *not* a strong predictor of performance."[282] In other words, for a biologically male body that has already undergone puberty, testosterone's effects on body development are already complete; hormone therapy that reduces testosterone levels going forward does little to reduce the built-in biological advantage that has already developed.

And to be clear, the collegiate opportunities for women impacted by transgender ideology are by no means limited to athletics. Males identifying as females can also harm women and girls by seeking positions set aside for women in STEM fields, on boards of directors, and in other areas.[283] They can apply for and win many scholarships that

---

[280] Ibid.

[281] Ibid.

[282] Ibid.; emphasis added, citations omitted.

[283] For representative STEM and business opportunities reserved for women, see, for example: "Amazon Shows STEM Opportunities to Caledonia HS Girls," *WoodTV*, March 23, 2022, https://www.woodtv.com/video/amazon-shows-stem-opportunities-to-caledonia-hs-girls/7543892/, https://perma.cc/7MNM-CP7Q in which Amazon gives ten female students an opportunity to contemplate future careers in STEM; and

are set aside exclusively for women.[284] They can take honorifics re-
served for women, such as *USA Today*'s "Woman of the Year" award.[285]
And they can even seize game show titles like *Jeopardy*'s "Winningest
Woman."[286] So much for willing the good of women.

Many Church officials see the issue of harm even more broadly.
When the issue of male athletes competing in women's sports arose
in Nebraska in early 2016, Nebraska's bishops, Archbishop George
J. Lucas of Omaha, Bishop James D. Conley of Lincoln, and Bishop
Joseph G. Hanefeldt of Grand Island, released a joint statement
against the proposal. They focused not just on the fundamental
unfairness to student athletes but on how gender ideology would
negatively impact human development and families: "It would be
unjust to allow a harmful and deceptive gender ideology to shape
either what is taught or how activities are conducted in our
schools," they explained. "This would certainly have a negative

Jessica Guynn, "This California Law Got Companies to Add Record
Numbers of Women to Their Corporate Boards," *USA Today*, February 21,
2022, https://www.usatoday.com/story/money/2022/02/21/california-
women-board-seats-gender-diversity-quota/6852554001/?gnt-cfr=1,
https://perma.cc/JM34-CY73 which notes the record number of women
added to company boards headquartered in California after the state set
quotas for women board membership.

[284] For a list of academic scholarships reserved for women, see, for example:
"Scholarships for Women," *Scholarships.com*, https://www.scholarships.
com/financial-aid/college-scholarships/scholarships-by-type/scholar-
ships-for-women/. https://perma.cc/2V3L-YXFK

[285] Suzette Hackney, "Women of the Year: Rachel Levine," *USA Today*, March
13, 2022, https://www.usatoday.com/in-depth/opinion/2022/03/13/
rachel-levine-honoree-usa-today-women-of-the-year/6600134001/.
https://perma.cc/R3FW-ZHVB

[286] Reis Thebault, "'Jeopardy!' Champ Amy Schneider's 21st Win in a Row
Makes Her the Show's Winningest Woman," *The Washington Post*, December 29, 2021, https://www.washingtonpost.com/arts-entertain-
ment/2021/12/29/amy-schneider-jeopardy-record/. https://perma.
cc/W8D7-VYXV

impact on students' and society's attitudes towards the fundamental nature of the human person and the human family."[287]

The Nebraska bishops also quoted Pope Francis's June 8, 2015 address to the bishops of Puerto Rico, in which he made clear that "the complementarity of man and woman, the pinnacle of the divine creation, is being questioned by the so-called gender ideology, in the name of a more free and just society. The differences between man and woman are not for opposition or subordination, but for communion and generation, always in the 'image and likeness' of God."[288]

Privacy spaces

On May 13, 2016, the U.S. Department of Justice and Education sent an extraordinary "Dear Colleague" letter to the nation's schools. The letter explained that Title IX — which sensibly requires schools to maintain separate showers, restrooms, and locker rooms for men and women — now required schools to allow access to such facilities based on "an individual's internal sense of gender." Refusal to capitulate risked losing federal funding.[289] Although that letter was subsequently rescinded by the following presidential administration, numerous school districts used it to justify changing their policies

---

[287] Bishop Joseph G. Hanefeldt, Archbishop George J. Lucas, Bishop James D. Conley, "Statement on the Nebraska School Activities Association's Policy on Transgender Student Participation," *Catholic Culture*, January 4, 2016, https://www.catholicculture.org/culture/library/view.cfm?recnum=11128. https://perma.cc/22CR-2LZD

[288] Lauretta Brown, "Catholic Bishops: Don't Let Biological Males Participate as Girls in Girls' Sports," *CNSNews*, January 6, 2016, https://cnsnews.com/news/article/Lauretta-brown/Nebraska-bishops-warn-against-harmful-and-deceptive-gender-ideology. https://perma.cc/Y8AK-QBJG

[289] U.S. Department of Justice, Civil Rights Division, and U.S. Department of Education, Office for Civil Rights, "Dear Colleague Letter on Transgender Students," May 13, 2016, available at https://bit.ly/2kQOcUa. https://perma.cc/CQ7Z-UYNT

for privacy spaces. In those districts, sex is no longer the determining factor for who has access to the male and female showers; instead, self-professed "gender identity" is.

Unsurprisingly, such policies have created problems. In the 2016–2017 school year, Boyertown Area School District in Pennsylvania adopted such a policy and did not notify students or parents of this change. One male student, "Joel Doe," found out in an embarrassing way — clad only in his underwear in the men's locker room, he encountered a female student wearing nothing above her waist except her bra. Another student, Alexis Lightcap, encountered a male student in the women's restroom and, as caught on video, was so shocked that she fled.[290]

When the students went to school officials and learned about the policy, officials instructed them to "tolerate" the new arrangement and try to make it seem "natural."[291] The consequences were predictable. Some students stopped changing in the locker rooms, where partial and full nudity were common. Joel Doe was penalized in gym class for not changing into gym clothes. Joel eventually left the school entirely and missed his senior year at Boyertown.[292] School officials gave short shrift to other students' privacy interests, concluding that "a female student ... has *no expectation of privacy* from a [male professing to be a] female when using ... the bathrooms or locker rooms."[293]

When the students sued, a federal judge dismissed the suit, concluding that it was wrong to consider the female student who

---

[290] Doe v. Boyertown Area School District, U.S. No. 18-658, Petition for a Writ of Certiorari (November 19, 2018), 2, 6–7; available at https://www.supremecourt.gov/DocketPDF/18/18-658/72545/20181119143351462_Boyertown%20Cert%20Petition%20Final.pdf. https://perma.cc/96F4-VB68

[291] Ibid., 7.

[292] Ibid.

[293] Ibid., 8; emphasis added.

Joel encountered in the locker room as anything other than a male wearing a bra. On appeal, a panel of three federal judges reached the same conclusion.

The panel said that the school's policy promoted "inclusivity, acceptance, and tolerance" and benefited all students by promoting acceptance.[294] That *sounds* like a policy that desires the good of all students. But by definition, the policy did not benefit the students who were made uncomfortable enough to sue. Indeed, the plaintiff students had actually reduced water intake and fasted to reduce how frequently they needed to go to the restroom, so as to minimize or avoid encountering opposite-sex students.

And this is not just a school problem. The Downtown Soup Kitchen Hope Center is a Christian non-profit in Anchorage, Alaska that offers job-skills training, meals, clothing, and other necessities for homeless men and women. It also offers a free overnight shelter for women. Because many of the shelter residents are escaping from abusive situations, the Hope Center allows only women to stay overnight. It's the kind of ministry that government officials typically support.

But in January 2018, a biological man who identified as a woman tried to access the overnight women's shelter. He would have been sleeping in a common room mere feet away from women, many of whom had been trafficked, abused, or sexually assaulted by men. He was intoxicated and injured, so the Hope Center referred him to a local hospital and paid a cab to take him there. But the man filed a complaint with the Anchorage Equal Rights Commission, alleging that the Center discriminated against him based on his professed "gender identity."

In the end, it took a federal court order to stop the city from using a nondiscrimination law to shut down the Center because of its women-only overnight policy. Otherwise, city officials would have

[294] Ibid., 9–12.

insisted that this Christian homeless shelter support the city's gender policies at the expense of the vulnerable women the Center serves.[295]

California has also put gender ideology ahead of women's safety: a California law allows biological males who identify as females to transfer to women's prisons. Unsurprisingly, this policy has "led to multiple sexual assaults of female inmates, physical attacks, and widespread 'psychological distress' in women's prisons, according to a lawsuit."[296] Incredibly, the California law, enacted as SB 132, requires the California Department of Corrections to "house transgender, gender-nonconforming and intersex (TGI) individuals in a manner that matches their identity," no matter their anatomy — no hormones or surgeries required.[297]

Since the policy's enactment, "hundreds of men have applied for transfers to women's prisons, and dozens have already been transferred," resulting in "intimidation, sexual harassment, physical assaults, and sexual assaults committed by the men against female inmates."[298] Gender activists decry the plaintiffs' claims as "echo[ing] right-wing depictions of trans women as sexual predators."[299] But the allegations regarding the assaults and harassment remain.

---

[295] Order, The Downtown Soup Kitchen d/b/a Downtown Hope Center v. Municipality of Anchorage, No. 3:18-cv-00190-SLG (D. Alaska August 9, 2019); available at https://adflegal.org/sites/default/files/2022-07/Downtown-Hope-Center-v.-Municipality-of-Anchorage-I-2019-08-09-Order-Regarding-Pending-Motions.pdf. https://perma.cc/LP5A-Q48V

[296] Raymond Wolfe, "California's Transgender Policies Led to Sexual Assaults, Harassment of Female Prisoners, Lawsuit Says," LifeSite, November 18, 2021, https://www.lifesitenews.com/news/californias-transgender-policies-led-to-sexual-assaults-traumatization-of-female-prisoners-lawsuit-says/. https://perma.cc/5V93-4PLW

[297] Ibid.

[298] Ibid.

[299] "TERF Inmates Sue California for Placing Transgender Women in Female Prisons," LGBTQNation, November 26, 2021, https://www.lgbtqnation.com/2021/11/terf-inmates-sue-california-placing-transgender-women-female-prisons/. https://perma.cc/UQM5-YXJB

Nevertheless, transgender prison policy has now gone national: President Biden's Department of Justice has released new guidance — reversing the previous federal rules — that now allows male inmates who identify as transgender to be housed with female inmates and requires prison officials to use inmates' preferred pronouns.[300] Respect and dignity for female inmates demands a more compassionate response.

Free speech and employment

Dr. Nicholas Meriwether has been a philosophy professor at Shawnee State University in Portsmouth, Ohio, for twenty-five years. He served in the university's faculty senate, designed a philosophy and religion bachelor's degree program, taught a generation of students, and had a spotless disciplinary record. He is also a Christian who believes that "God created human beings as either male or female, that this sex is fixed in each person from the moment of conception, and that it cannot be changed, regardless of an individual's feelings or desires." He also believes that he cannot "affirm as true ideas and concepts that are not true." Doing so would be harmful to his students.

But Dr. Meriwether's world was turned upside down when the university adopted a policy requiring faculty to refer to students by preferred pronouns. A male student in his political philosophy course approached Dr. Meriwether after class and "demanded" that Dr. Meriwether use "feminine titles and pronouns" when referring to the student. When Dr. Meriwether paused to think about that request, the student became hostile, circling around Dr. Meriwether, calling the professor a vulgar word, approaching in a threatening manner, and promising to get Dr. Meriwether fired if he did not comply.

---

[300] Ryan Foley, "Biden to Allow Trans-Identified Men in Women's Prisons, Reversing Trump-Era Ban 'Except in Rare Cases,'" *Christian Post*, January 31, 2022, https://www.christianpost.com/news/biden-to-allow-trans-identified-men-in-womens-prisons.html. https://perma.cc/7VUA-QM4Z

Dr. Meriwether's dean advised him to refrain from using sex-based references — such as "he," "she," "Mr.," or "Ms." Even though following this suggestion would be difficult, given that Dr. Meriwether uses the Socratic method, which involves a lot of class conversation, Dr. Meriwether proposed that he continue using pronouns but refer to the disgruntled student using only the student's last name. The Dean accepted that compromise; the student did not. So the university changed its position too and insisted that Dr. Meriwether use the student's preferred pronouns.

Attempting to find common ground with the university, Dr. Meriwether inquired whether he could use preferred pronouns in class but explain his views in his course syllabus, "noting that he was [using preferred pronouns] under compulsion [while] setting forth his personal and religious beliefs about gender identity," i.e., that God created us male and female. The university rejected that possible proposal and, after a formal investigation, placed a written warning in Dr. Meriwether's file that stated further corrective actions could be imposed if he violated the policy again — up to and including termination. Fortunately, a federal court of appeals preliminarily recognized that the university's treatment of Dr. Meriwether violated his free speech rights.[301] The case concluded with a settlement favorable to Dr. Meriwether that allows him to continue teaching at the university without violating his conscience.[302]

Again, this incident is hardly isolated. A high school in Virginia fired Peter Vlaming, a high school French teacher, because he refused the school's demand that he use male pronouns when referring to a female student. Because Mr. Vlaming believes as a matter of religious

---

[301] Meriwether v. Hartop, 992 F.3d 492 (2021).

[302] "Victory: Shawnee State Agrees Professors Can't Be Forced to Speak Contrary to Their Beliefs," *Alliance Defending Freedom*, April 14, 2022, https://adfmedia.org/case/meriwether-v-trustees-shawnee-state-university. https://perma.cc/M37T-T5CQ

conviction and human anatomy that sex is biologically set and can't be changed, he believes that it would be lying to refer to a female student using male pronouns. It would also be expressing ideas that Mr. Vlaming considers false: namely, that "gender identity, rather than biological reality, fundamentally shapes and defines who we truly are as humans, that our sex can change, and that a woman who identifies as a man *really is* a man."[303]

Mr. Vlaming tried to accommodate and respect the student without violating his own conscience. For example, upon learning that the student wished to be called by a name that is culturally masculine, Mr. Vlaming allowed the entire French class to pick new names that semester so the student would not stand out. Mr. Vlaming also always tried to use the student's name to avoid the use of pronouns. But ultimately, the school demanded that Mr. Vlaming comply with the student's desire to be addressed by masculine pronouns. When he could not, he was fired — not for anything he did affirmatively, but merely for what he would not say. Although students protested the firing of their beloved teacher with a walkout, the school was uncompromising.[304]

A similar situation involves high school orchestra teacher John Kluge. His school, too, insisted that its teachers affirm transgender ideology by using students' preferred names and pronouns. Like Mr. Vlaming, Mr. Kluge believes as a matter of religion and a matter of biology that "following the district's policy would require him to tell a dangerous lie to his students." He asked for and received an accommodation: to call all of his students by last name only, like a coach, allowing him to focus on teaching music while staying neutral regarding gender ideology.

---

[303] Vlaming v. West Point School Board, et al. Virginia Supreme Court No. 211061, Petition for Appeal (November 12, 2021), 5; available at https://adflegal.org/sites/default/files/2021-11/Vlaming-v-West-Point-School-Board-Petition-for-Appeal-2021-11-12.pdf. https://perma.cc/5X8T-V8DM

[304] Ibid., 6–13.

At first, the school considered that request reasonable and granted it. But after a few teachers and students complained, the school pressured Mr. Kluge to leave his position voluntarily. When he declined, the school took away the accommodation, said there would be no exceptions to the policy, and forced Mr. Kluge to quit or be terminated.[305]

Dr. Allan Josephson faced a similar fate for a different reason. For nearly fifteen years, he built and served as Division Chief of the University of Louisville's Division of Child and Adolescent Psychiatry, helping the department to become nationally renowned. But in October 2017, Dr. Josephson participated in a panel discussion about gender dysphoria at the Heritage Foundation, a Washington, D.C. think tank. Dr. Josephson's comments led the University of Louisville effectively to fire him. What do you suppose he said to elicit such a harsh response?

"Dr. Josephson expressed his view that medical professionals should seek to understand and treat the psychological issues that often cause this confusion, rather than rushing children into more radical, aggressive treatments, like puberty-blocking drugs and cross-sex hormones." In addition, relying on his thirty-five years of experience as a psychiatrist, "Dr. Josephson argued that children are not mature enough to make permanent, life-altering decisions of any kind, let alone medical ones such as this." As noted above, "80 to 95 percent of children who say they experience gender dysphoria naturally come to accept their biological sex over time."

It did not matter that Dr. Josephson's comments were supported by scientific research and were made in the best interests of children. It did not matter that he was expressing his personal views and not the

---

[305] Kluge v. Brownsburg Community School Corp., 7th Circuit Court, No. 21-2475, Appellant's Opening Brief (July 12, 2021), 4–5; available at https://adflegal.org/sites/default/files/2021-10/Kluge-v-Brownsburg-Community-School-Co-Opening-Brief-10-1-21.pdf. https://perma.cc/X7GB-LVUN

views of the university. It did not matter that he had thirty-five years of experience or even that this event was not on campus. Within weeks, "Dr. Josephson was demoted to the role of a junior faculty member." And in February of 2019, the university told Dr. Josephson that it was not going to renew his contract.[306] We cannot allow individuals like Dr. Josephson, who simply speak the truth, to be silenced.

Silencing of medical professionals

As already discussed at length, there is substantial medical and scientific evidence that supports the Church's teachings regarding gender ideology and the dignity of every human person. But far too often, gender activists respond to this data with public attacks, smearing those who disagree with them as haters and bigots.

Consider Dr. Paul McHugh. He has served for forty years as the University Distinguished Service Professor of Psychiatry at Johns Hopkins Medical School; for twenty-six of these years, he served as the Psychiatrist-in-Chief of Johns Hopkins Hospital. After initially pioneering sex-change surgery for those who identified as transgender, Johns Hopkins closed its gender clinic in the 1970s after Dr. McHugh determined "that the practice brought no important benefits." He encourages doctors to treat those with gender dysphoria with "evidence-based care," and he condemns the cultural and media promotion of the "idea that one's sex is fluid and a matter open to choice." "It is doing much damage to families, adolescents, and children and should be confronted as an opinion without biological foundation wherever it emerges," he says.[307]

---

[306] "A University Effectively Fired This Professor After He Spoke about Gender Dysphoria," *Alliance Defending Freedom*, November 18, 2019, https://adflegal.org/blog/university-effectively-fired-professor-after-he-spoke-conservative-think-tank. https://perma.cc/V7EE-6R82

[307] Paul McHugh, "Transgenderism: A Pathogenic Meme," *Public Discourse*, June 10, 2015, https://thepublicdiscourse.com/2015/06/15145/. https://perma.cc/KSP4-HU8J

For taking these positions, which are in fact backed by scientific observations and data, Dr. McHugh, now ninety-two years old, has been on transgender advocates' "enemies list" for a long time.[308] The Southern Poverty Law Center accuses him of holding "anti-trans views" and of being a "conservative" — although he has identified as a Democrat — criticizing him for arguing that "trans people should be treated as disordered, like people with anorexia nervosa."[309] The Human Rights Campaign smears Dr. McHugh as the "go-to 'expert' for anti-equality extremists" who publishes "hateful and damaging essays."[310]

Another influential expert in this field is Dr. Paul W. Hruz, an Associate Professor of Pediatrics and Associate Professor of Cellular Biology at Washington University of Medicine in St. Louis. He has made many public presentations, submitted numerous legal briefs to courts, and, along with Drs. Lawrence Mayer and Paul McHugh, has published a groundbreaking article explaining that the use of puberty blockers to treat gender dysphoria is a "drastic and experimental measure."[311]

Yet when Dr. Hruz agreed to present at a 2020 forum in a Catholic parish on the topic of "Sex and Gender: In Light of Truth,

[308] Matthew J. Franck and Paul McHugh, "A Rosy-Cheeked Irish Boy Who Has Come Very Far: An Interview with Dr. Paul McHugh," *Public Discourse*, May 20, 2021, https://thepublicdiscourse.com/2021/05/75886/. https://perma.cc/NGZ2-TFZ7

[309] Hatewatch Staff, "Anti-LGBT Hate Group Releases Anti-Trans Position Statement," *SPLC*, April 7, 2016, https://www.splcenter.org/hatewatch/2016/04/07/anti-lgbt-hate-group-releases-anti-trans-position-statement. https://perma.cc/6B8G-ENQ8

[310] Sarah McBride, "McHugh Exposed: HRC Launches Website Debunking the Junk Science of Paul McHugh," *Human Rights Campaign*, April 21, 2017, https://www.hrc.org/press-releases/mchugh-exposed-hrc-launches-website-debunking-the-junk-science-of-paul-mchu. https://perma.cc/GB4J-UEQL

[311] Paul Hruz, Lawrence S. Mayer, and Paul R. McHugh, "Growing Pains: Problems with Puberty Suppression in Treating Gender Dysphoria," *The New Atlantis* 52 (Spring 2017): 3–36; available at thenewatlantis.com/publications/growing-pains. https://perma.cc/8RUH-4YUV

Beauty and Goodness," an LGBTQIA+ advocacy group accused Dr. Hruz of being "detrimental" to the progress of transgender health by "blurring the lines between religious freedom and medicine," characterizing Dr. Hruz's presentation of the issues as "transphobic rhetoric" that is "dangerous to the Transgender Community."[312] The group did not proffer any counter scientific evidence; it merely proclaimed: "We as an organization oppose his ideology."[313] The Southern Poverty Law Center maligned him as one of many "crackpots ... at the medical fringe."[314]

It is not just doctors and scientists whom gender activists want to silence. They also want to censor therapists who merely want to help those struggling with gender dysphoria to work through their underlying issues.

For example, the State of Washington in 2018 enacted a law that aims to ban any listening or talking between minor individuals and a counselor of choice that seeks to help the client achieve comfort with her or his biological sex. The ban includes minor clients who *want* this kind of counseling so that they can live according to the teachings of their faith. This law threatens the professional licenses and businesses of counselors like Brian Tingley, who has helped countless Washington clients over a twenty-year period to achieve the goals that his clients themselves set. Now, if Brian has even one such discussion with a minor client, even one who transitioned and now desires to detransition, the State of

---

[312] "Pride St. Louis Statement on Dr. Paul Hruz," *PrideSTL*, January 16, 2020, https://www.pridestl.org/pressrelease/2020116. https://perma. cc/K87L-PRVX

[313] Ibid.

[314] David Cary Hart, "Alliance Defending Freedom Developed a Stable of Anti-LBGT 'Expert' Witnesses," *SPLC*, December 13, 2017, https://www. splcenter.org/hatewatch/2017/12/13/alliance-defending-freedom-developed-stable-anti-lgbt-expert-witnesses. https://perma.cc/A352-PVGR

Washington could fine him up to $5,000 and suspend or revoke his license to practice.[315]

Similar laws have been enacted in other states and localities — though a federal court of appeals has recently said that these types of laws violate the First Amendment's guarantee of free speech. Striking down Florida city and county ordinances that ban therapists from engaging in counseling intended to change a minor's gender expression or identity (among other things), the court recognized that "the First Amendment has no carveout for controversial speech." "People have intense moral, religious, and spiritual views about these matters — on all sides," said the court. "And that is exactly why the First Amendment does not allow communities to determine how their neighbors may be counseled about matters of sexual orientation or gender."[316] Nevertheless, until the U.S. Supreme Court weighs in, these laws will continue to proliferate and cause harm to those who seek counseling.

The withering of parental rights

Free speech in the context of counseling is not the only form of discussion that gender activists have tried to suppress. Open communication has also been censored in schools.

Schoolteachers and staff should never keep secrets from parents about the parents' children. Yet that is exactly what happened in Madison, Wisconsin, where a school district decided to cut parents out of the loop if a child begins identifying as transgender.

In 2018, the Madison Metropolitan School District adopted a new policy requiring staff to address students with transgender names and pronouns if a child requests it, without parental knowledge or

[315] "Tingley v. Ferguson: Summary," *Alliance Defending Freedom*, https://adflegal.org/case/tingley-v-ferguson. https://perma.cc/JUB9-DBRK

[316] Otto v. City of Boca Raton, 11th Circuit Court, 981 f.3d 854, 859, 871 (2020).

consent — and sometimes "behind parents' backs" — with the goal of "disrupting the gender binary." Specifically, the policy "requires teachers to actively deceive parents about their child's gender identity disorder by using the child's 'transgender' name at school, but using the child's true name in front of his or her parents."[317]

If this sounds oppressive and nightmarish, that's because it is. But frighteningly, it is hardly an isolated incident. In Florida, parents were forced to file a lawsuit against the Leon County School Board in federal court to challenge a similar policy. After the parents informed their thirteen-year-old daughter's middle school that she was undergoing counseling for gender confusion, they gave permission for school employees to use a nickname but strictly prohibited any other social transition such as preferred pronouns or allowing the daughter to use male privacy spaces. Yet over the next month, school employees referred to their daughter using they/them pronouns, solicited her preferences for which bathroom to use, and asked if she wanted to sleep with the boys on an overnight school trip. When the parents requested more information, school officials said that "by law," the parents were not entitled to information or input without their daughter's consent.[318]

After the parents made additional inquiries, school officials gave them the Leon County School's Lesbian, Gay, Bisexual, Transgender, Gender Nonconforming, and Questioning Support Guide. The Guide says that parents should not be informed if a "student has exhibited behavior in school leading administrators or teachers to believe the student is LGBTQ+" because some parents are "unaccepting," so

---

[317] "Wisconsin School District Tried to Lie to Parents," *Alliance Defending Freedom*, March 10, 2022, https://adflegal.org/article/court-stops-wisconsin-school-district-lying-parents. https://perma.cc/NSW7-HEJP

[318] Mary Laval, "Breaking News: Florida Parents Sue School for Hiding Child's Trans-Identification," *Genspect*, https://genspect.org/breaking-news-florida-parents-sue-school-for-hiding-childs-trans-identification/. https://perma.cc/VF5S-8ETK

disclosure can "expose" the student "to physical and emotional harm."[319] The Guide also instructs that "any student may use restroom and locker room facilities in accordance with their gender identity."[320]

In California, the California Teachers Association distributed a packet that provides an "instructional guide" for teachers to propagandize students with gay and transgender information. The guide recommends that teachers recruit students *ten years old or younger* to join and lead LGBTQ clubs. It also urges teachers to ask students their "Kinsey Scale" rating (named for Alfred Kinsey, the discredited sex researcher), which purports to evaluate a person's sexual orientation and sexuality based on their answers to questions about sexual desires and interests. Among other things, the tool asks the young children answering these questions to describe how they feel about having sex with someone of the same sex and other sex fantasies. The packet recommends videos such as "Coming Out GAY to My 5 Year Old Brother," an animated music video called "Everyone is Gay," and the *First Person* YouTube channel, which has content such as "Growing Up Intersex," "Asexuality," and "The Importance of Being Cliterate." The packet also encourages the clubs to honor confidentiality — "What is said here, stays here" is one of the ground rules — so that parents won't be informed about what's going on.[321]

When it comes to parental rights and gender ideology, certain school administrators are not the only officials trying to step between

[319] Leon County Schools, "Inclusive School Guide for LCS Employees," 15, https://tallahasseereports.com/wp-content/uploads/2022/04/Draft-Guide.pdf. https://perma.cc/6D67-CMM3

[320] Ibid., 14.

[321] Christopher Tremoglie, "Leaked Documents Show How Teachers Recruit Students, Form Gay and Transgender Clubs in Schools," *Washington Examiner*, March 30, 2022, https://www.washingtonexaminer.com/opinion/leaked-documents-show-how-teachers-recruit-students-form-gay-and-transgender-clubs-in-schools. https://perma.cc/6KCX-BW9S

parents and their children. Parents who prefer watchful waiting to immediate affirmation and transition may find themselves before a judge.

Take Ted Hudacko, a California father of two and an Apple senior software engineer. After Ted's wife announced that she was divorcing him and that her son was transgender, Ted found himself in court, defending not only his right to shared custody but even his right to see his son at all. The judge — who had not disclosed that she had "celebrated" her own child's gender transition to either the parties or their lawyers — asked Ted whether he would love his son if the son "believed himself to be the Queen of England." She also expressed concern about the fact that Ted thought his son "might" not truly be transgender but was merely confused.[322]

The judge initially granted Ted's ex-wife sole custody of their son on a temporary basis and appointed a "minor's counsel" to investigate the son's welfare before a permanent decision was made. The counsel dismissed Ted's expert counselor—who recommended the approach of watchful waiting for children who presented with gender dysphoria—as a "crank." The counsel's preferred expert was "a leading advocate of the affirmation-only approach." Abigail Shrier explains what happened next:

> Within just a few months, the court would definitively end Ted's parental relationship. He would have no right to see [his son], no right to talk to him, no right to demand that [his son] attend therapy with him, and absolutely no right to stop a medical transition already planned by the Child and Adolescent Gender Center of UCSF Benioff Children's Hospital.[323]

[322] Abigail Shrier, "Child Custody's Gender Gauntlet: Courts Are Adopting Gender Ideology, Parents are Paying the Price," *The Truth Fairy*, February 7, 2022, https://abigailshrier.substack.com/p/child-custodys-gender-gauntlet. https://perma.cc/876P-9XKQ

[323] Ibid.

Ted is hardly alone. Parents in Arizona lost custody of their fifteen-year-old daughter when they could not agree that she was "actually" a boy. After the fact, one of the lawyers involved was able to obtain from the judge the training sessions that the entire court had received from gender activists. These included four transparently one-sided presentations and lunch meetings with the "LGBTQ Court-Involved Youth Committee." Every judge on the court likely took part in these trainings and luncheons, with "no indication" that they heard from a doctor or scientist with a contrary view, much less from a detransitioner.[324]

The stealthy infiltration by gender ideologists of our nation's most important educational and political institutions, from schools to courts, is alarming and has caused widespread harm to individuals, families, and communities. But the problem is even larger: nearly all our cultural institutions also have been taken over by gender activists. In the following chapter, we will examine how these institutions promote propaganda that harms many.

---

[324] Ibid.

CHAPTER 9

Cultural Attacks on Human Sexuality

♀ ♂

WHEN A SOCIETY, AND a culture, has lost fundamental truth and pursues a false and dangerous ideology, it has also lost its way. This chapter will catalogue how gender ideology is pervading every aspect of our culture, from children's television shows to coercive social-media platforms. It will discuss how public-accommodation laws are being used to try to force Catholic hospitals and doctors to violate the Church's Ethical and Religious Directives for Catholic Health Care Services and to compel employers to provide insurance coverage for gender-transition surgery in health plans. It will also examine how the federal government is responding to cultural factors by forcing gender ideology on public schools and places of employment.

When we witness such lies being promoted in our culture, there is only one appropriate loving response: we must speak about God's plan for human sexuality with charity and truth. Yet choosing how and where to do that can be challenging. Mass media and popular culture have tried to censor and silence religious organizations and individuals when they speak out on the importance of gender ideology, from the *New York Times*'s attack on the Vatican's *Male and Female He Created Them* to the removal of Ryan T. Anderson's important book, *When Harry Became Sally*, from Amazon. Sad to say, there is very little true love being displayed by any of these powerful institutions. But we must confront their lies with the truth, and their hatred and attempts to silence with love and dialogue.

Media and entertainment

In 2015, five of the U.S. Supreme Court's nine Justices decided *Obergefell v. Hodges* and "found" a constitutional right to same-sex marriage in the Due Process Clause of the Fourteenth Amendment.[325] This amendment says nothing about the definition of marriage. It says only that Americans are entitled to "due process," which typically means the right to a hearing in front of an impartial judge and similar procedural rights. This was a remarkable turnaround. Only four decades earlier, in 1972, the Court had rejected a request to hear an identical case — plaintiffs claiming a federal constitutional right to same-sex marriage — "for want of a substantial federal question."[326] In other words, in 1972, the Court unanimously concluded that the U.S. Constitution had nothing to say about the question of how to define marriage; in 2015, the Court discovered a new right in the same constitutional silence.

What does this have to do with gender ideology in media and entertainment? Everything. It was the incredible transformation in public opinion about same-sex relationships that made *Obergefell* possible. And that transformation was led by the media and entertainment industries.

In an article issued shortly after *Obergefell*, the *Los Angeles Times* confessed in a headline: "Years Before Court Ruling, Pop Culture

---

[325] Obergefell v. Hodges, 576 U.S. 644 (2015).
[326] *Baker v. Nelson*, 409 U.S. 810, 810 (1972).

Shaped Same-Sex Marriage Debate."[327] The article pointed to Tom Hanks's award-winning role as a gay lawyer dying of AIDS in the movie *Philadelphia*; a housemate who had AIDS on MTV's *The Real World* series; and popular television shows like *Queer Eye for the Straight Guy, Ellen, Will & Grace,* and *Modern Family*.[328] All of this entertainment content normalized same-sex conduct that the Church, from its inception, has considered contrary to God's laws regarding human sexuality and that Western civilization (and indeed, almost all other civilizations) had until very recently widely condemned. The newspaper even quoted NBC Entertainment's chairman, who identified as gay, as being "surprised" the Supreme Court's "decision wasn't more one-sided because public opinion already seemed to be overwhelmingly there."[329]

The same playbook is being used today to promote the transgender movement. The Supreme Court issued its long-expected same-sex marriage decision in June 2015. Only two months earlier, Olympic gold medalist Bruce Jenner announced he was a "trans woman" in a *20/20* interview with Diane Sawyer. Less than two weeks before the Supreme Court's decision, Jenner debuted a new name and image — using the name Caitlyn Jenner — and began using feminine pronouns publicly as self-descriptors.[330]

The following month, in July 2015, the TLC network debuted *I Am Jazz*, a reality television show about Jazz Jennings, who, as discussed in chapter six, was born male but supposedly began

---

[327] Scott Collins and Meredith Blake, "Years Before Court Ruling, Pop Culture Shaped Same-Sex Marriage Debate," *Los Angeles Times*, June 27, 2015, https://www.latimes.com/entertainment/la-et-st-0628-media-gay-marriage-20150628-story.html. https://perma.cc/7PCE-4ED8

[328] Ibid.

[329] Ibid.

[330] *Wikipedia, The Free Encyclopedia*, s.v. "Caitlyn Jenner," https://en.wikipedia.org/wiki/Caitlyn_Jenner#Coming_out_as_a_transgender_woman. https://perma.cc/7W7U-8XVM

identifying as a girl at age two. The series features Jazz and his family "dealing with typical teen drama through the lens of a transgender youth" and has continued for at least eight seasons. Jazz has been in the media spotlight since 2007, when the then-six-year-old interviewed with Barbara Walters to discuss the child's "gender identity."[331] In addition to the show, Jazz published a children's book, *I Am Jazz*, designed for teachers and parents to read to young children (ages four through eight, according to Amazon.com). The book has received multiple awards, including the 2015 American Library Association's Rainbow Project Book List Award.[332] As for the many problems Jazz experienced after his transition surgery (also discussed in chapter six) — well, the media and entertainment industries tend to downplay those details.

If you're a television fan, you've likely noticed that trans or "nonbinary" characters are appearing more frequently. Indeed, it is getting difficult to turn on the television *without* catching a show that has a transgender theme. The list of transgender characters is growing quickly and includes shows such as *Glee, The Bold and the Beautiful, Law & Order: Special Victims Unit, Two and a Half Men, Twin Peaks, CSI: Crime Scene Investigation, The Closer, How to Get Away with Murder, Chicago Med, Ugly Betty, Grey's Anatomy, Star Trek: Discovery*, and many others.[333] Wikipedia lists more than two hundred "transgender-related films,"[334] and the venerable *Good*

[331] *Wikipedia, The Free Encyclopedia*, s.v. "I Am Jazz," https://en.wikipedia.org/wiki/I_Am_Jazz. https://perma.cc/3PZR-4LAP

[332] *Wikipedia, The Free Encyclopedia*, s.v. "I Am Jazz (book)," https://en.wikipedia.org/wiki/I_Am_Jazz_(book). https://perma.cc/CE8S-4K3E

[333] *Wikipedia, The Free Encyclopedia*, s.v. "List of transgender characters in television," https://en.wikipedia.org/wiki/List_of_transgender_characters_in_television. https://perma.cc/F6VR-6X9X

[334] *Wikipedia, The Free Encyclopedia*, Category: Transgender-Related Films, https://en.wikipedia.org/wiki/Category:Transgender-related_films. https://perma.cc/EPL9-ZC4V

Housekeeping recently published an article recommending the "15 Best Transgender Movies to Watch Right Now."[335]

The *I Am Jazz* children's book also shows that there is no age limit for gender-ideology indoctrination. In a recent episode of *Muppet Babies*, a television show for children ages four through seven, Gonzo, who has always been recognized as a male character, makes the decision to become a "princess" and wear a dress, though only after keeping this decision a secret. When Miss Piggy asks Gonzo why he didn't tell his friends, he responds, "Because you all expected me to look a certain way," and "I don't want you to be upset with me." This revelation causes Miss Piggy to apologize and say it "wasn't very nice" of Gonzo's friends "to tell you what to wear."[336]

Another popular children's television show, *Blue's Clues*, a combination live action and cartoon show intended for children as young as three years old,[337] released an episode to celebrate "Pride Month" in 2021. The episode featured a cartoon Pride Parade with a drag queen voiced by Nina West, a contestant from *RuPaul's Drag Race*. As each float goes by to the tune of "The Ants Go Marching One By One," West sings words encouraging viewers "to celebrate gay, lesbian, pansexual, transgender, non-binary, and bisexual parents." One float "featured a trans-identified beaver family" that included a beaver with "scars on its chest, apparently resulting from a

[335] Lizz Schumer, "15 Best Transgender Movies to Watch Right Now," *Good Housekeeping*, November 22, 2022, https://www.goodhousekeeping.com/life/entertainment/g36107109/trans-movies-documentaries/. https://perma.cc/GUJ6-LCSN

[336] Kennedy Unthank, "Disney Uses 'Muppet Babies' Show to Promote Transgender Ideology," *Daily Citizen*, August 3, 2021, https://dailycitizen.focusonthefamily.com/disney-uses-muppet-babies-show-to-promote-transgender-ideology/. https://perma.cc/X9R5-4XEU

[337] Joly Herman, "Blue's Clues TV Review," *Common Sense Media*, https://www.commonsensemedia.org/tv-reviews/blues-clues. https://perma.cc/GG7X-HXW7

double mastectomy surgery."[338] To remove any doubt about the show's intentions, a spokesperson for Nickelodeon, the show's producer, confirmed that the cartoon markings were, in facts, scars from "top surgery."[339]

If marketing a gender-ideology agenda to three-year-olds sounds like a bad idea, that's because it is. Maria Keffler, co-founder of Partners for Ethical Care and author of the book *Desist, Detrans, & Detox: Getting Your Child Out of the Gender Cult,* called the episode "disturbing" and explained:

> Pre-adolescent children do not nor should not have explicit knowledge about or driving interest in sex or gender identity. Ethical professionals who work with children have long recognized that when young children are conversant about sexual behaviors, this is strongly suggestive of having been introduced to such material by adults who do not have the child's best interests at heart.[340]

Keffler noted that introducing sexual materials to young children is an inappropriate grooming tactic.[341]

Similar indoctrination takes place in the adult news media. The most recent edition of the Associated Press Stylebook instructs journalists that "gender is not synonymous with sex. Gender refers to a person's social identity, while sex refers to biological characteristics."

[338] Milton Quintanilla, "Nickelodeon's *Blue's Clues & You* Releases Pride Parade Song Featuring Drag Queen Singing with Transgender, Non-Binary Animals," *Christian Headlines,* June 1, 2021, https://www.christianheadlines.com/contributors/milton-quintanilla/nickelodeons-blues-clues-and-you-releases-pride-parade-song-featuring-drag-queen-singing-with-transgender-non-binary-animals.html. https://perma.cc/2LWG-FUVR

[339] Dan Evon, "Fact Check: Did Blue's Clues Pride Parade Feature a Beaver with 'Top Scars'?" *Snopes,* June 2, 2021, https://www.snopes.com/fact-check/blues-clues-pride-beaver-top-scars/. https://perma.cc/5ER7-N2K4

[340] Quintanilla, "Nickelodeon's *Blue's Clues & You* Releases Pride Parade Song."

[341] Ibid.

Accordingly, the word "transgender" to describe an individual in a news story "does not require what are known as sex reassignment or gender confirmation procedures." In addition, the Stylebook instructs reporters to refer to transgender people only using "the name by which they live publicly."[342] So if an AP reporter is writing about the gold-medal winner of the 1976 Olympics decathlon, the article would reference "Caitlyn Jenner" as the men's decathlon winner. These instructions misunderstand that sex and gender are not separable.

Social media

Social-media platforms have eagerly signed on to the agenda of gender activists. As early as 2014, Facebook users were given "fifty different terms people can use to identify their gender, as well as three preferred pronoun choices: him, her, or them." Spokespeople for the company explained that the goal was to give "people more choices in how they describe themselves, such as androgynous, bi-gender, intersex, gender fluid, or transsexual." Facebook developed their list of terms "after consulting with leading gay and transgender activists," and unsurprisingly, "the company plans to continue working with them."[343] Over time, Facebook determined that even seventy gender identities were not enough to satisfy its users' demands, so it eventually eliminated identity choices altogether so that users could define their gender identities in their own words.

Also consider Snapchat, the most popular social-media platform for U.S. teenagers until very recently. In 2015, Snapchat created "Discover," a feature that allows publishers "to showcase short, ad-supported content."

[342] Nicole Schuman, "AP Style Updates: Diversity, Equity and Inclusion," *PR News*, August 18, 2021, https://www.prnewsonline.com/ap-style-diversity-equity-inclusion/. https://perma.cc/ZNW3-URFH

[343] "Facebook Expands Gender Options: Transgender Activists Hail 'Big Advance,'" *The Guardian*, February 14, 2014, https://www.theguardian.com/technology/2014/feb/13/transgender-facebook-expands-gender-options. https://perma.cc/QL2B-J984

Snapchat has complete editorial control over Discover's content, and gender-ideology content is common. Among other things, Snapchat has promoted the series *My Extraordinary Family*, which features one episode in which twin sisters became twin brothers, one of whom socially transitioned at only five years of age. One MTV Snapchat series, *Drag My Dad*, highlights "Bob the drag queen" as its host. Another popular group on Snapchat, "The Try Guys," recently featured an episode in which its male hosts tried on "extreme" Valentine's Day women's lingerie.[344]

Today's most popular social-media platform for teenagers, TikTok, follows suit. According to one analysis, TikTok videos featuring the hashtag #Trans have been watched more than twenty-six *billion* times. These videos frequently "feature young people documenting in a fun, light-hearted way the various stages of undergoing experimental hormones and irreversible, body-altering surgeries to appear more as the opposite sex." A spokesperson for the group "Transgender Trend" described TikTok as "hugely influential" and "full of videos that portray medical transition as cool and edgy." LGB Alliance's Kate Harris opined that it is "no coincidence that the growth of TikTok coincides exactly with the exponential growth of children presenting with gender dysphoria," noting that TikTok's transgender messaging frequently says, "Don't involve your parents," and gives children the impression "that it is easy to change sex and that it is the answer to all of your problems."[345]

Videos and media promoting gender ideology are easy to find largely because of Google's ubiquitous YouTube. Take, for example,

[344] Evita Duffy-Alfonso, "Snapchat Is a Transgender Propaganda and Grooming Machine," *The Federalist*, February 27, 2021, https://sexchangeregret.com/snapchat-is-a-transgender-propaganda-and-grooming-machine/. https://perma.cc/Q9JJ-79ZQ

[345] Brandon Showalter, "TikTok Is Enticing Kids into Having Trans Surgeries, Take Cross-Sex Hormones: Child Advocates Warn," *Christian Post*, December 27, 2021, https://www.christianpost.com/news/tiktok-enticing-kids-to-get-trans-surgeries-child-advocates-warn.html. https://perma.cc/J8CW-J25A

Chase Ross, a young man who was born in Canada and whose mother abandoned the family when Chase was only one year old. While he was watching cat videos on YouTube, Chase stumbled across a video of a person who claimed to be transgender. After "binging" on trans videos, Chase decided that he was transgender and started talking about it on YouTube. By the time he turned twenty-eight, Chase's transgender YouTube channel had more than ten million views with a regular audience of more than 160,000 subscribers.

The opportunities for social media to influence young people is limitless, and its approach is the exact opposite of love, substituting changed identity and quick medical interventions for truth, accompaniment, and lasting healing. But for those who want to speak and live the truth regarding human sexuality, the challenges are daunting.

Public-accommodation laws

In the United States, laws serve as a primary shaper of culture. Why is that? Cardinal Francis George explains: "In a country continuously being knit together from so many diverse cultural, religious, and linguistic threads, legal language most often creates the terms of our public discourse as Americans."[346] So the laws we adopt will have a great deal of influence on the debate over gender ideology.

Public-accommodation laws, sometimes referred to as civil-rights laws, exist in nearly every state and locality. They have an undeniably admirable purpose: to stamp out discrimination based on race, sex, and other protected characteristics by coffee houses, realtors, restaurants, and other places of business that serve the public. But recently, governments and private-party plaintiffs — with the assistance of the courts — have begun using these

---

[346] Cardinal Francis E. George, "The Law as a Carrier of Culture," *Catholic Culture*, November 5, 1998, https://www.catholicculture.org/culture/library/view.cfm?recnum=751. https://perma.cc/2NPF-2V85

commendable laws for a new purpose: to advance gender ideology. Worse, the gender ideology agenda frequently attacks the rights of religious believers.

Since 1857, the Sisters of Mercy having been providing health care to the community in Sacramento, California. The Sisters founded Mercy San Juan Medical Center, a Catholic hospital just outside the city, in 1867. Today, the hospital is owned by Dignity Health, a nonprofit whose mission is to further "the healing ministry of Jesus."[347] In 2016, a female patient who identifies as a man scheduled a hysterectomy. After discovering that the procedure was intended to remove healthy reproductive organs, Dignity Health declined to perform the surgery and referred the patient to a different hospital, where the surgery took place only three days later.[348] This action was consistent with the United States Conference of Catholic Bishops' Ethical and Religious Directives for Catholic Health Care Services, which prohibit elective sterilization and would allow a hysterectomy only if there is a "present and serious pathology" that necessitates the surgery.[349]

The patient sued, invoking a California public-accommodations law (the Unruh Civil Rights Act) that prohibits "sex" discrimination in the provision of health care services. After a California state trial court dismissed the case, a division of the California Court of Appeals reinstated it, concluding that the patient had stated a legal claim for sex discrimination because the hospital was willing to perform

---

[347] Dignity Health v. Minton, U.S. Supreme Court No. 19-1135, Petition for Certiorari, p. 6, https://www.supremecourt.gov/DocketPDF/19/19-1135/138108/20200313135600983_Dignity%20Health%20Petition.pdf. https://perma.cc/5RJA-HHKR

[348] Ibid., 9–10.

[349] Helen Alvaré, "Should a Catholic Hospital Be Forced to Participate in Transgender Surgery?" *Our Sunday Visitor*, November 8, 2021, https://www.osvnews.com/amp/2021/11/08/should-a-catholic-hospital-be-forced-to-participate-in-transgender-surgery/. https://perma.cc/AY8M-KR5F

medically necessary hysterectomies only on female patients who do not identify as transgender. It made no difference to the court that the hospital would not perform a hysterectomy on any healthy person, no matter how they identified. The California Supreme Court denied review, and only three U.S. Supreme Court Justices were willing to review, when four were needed. The case is far from over. But in the meantime, it jeopardizes the religious convictions of Catholic health care providers in a broad variety of contexts.[350]

Other examples abound. Sacred Heart Academy, a west Michigan Catholic school, was forced to sue the Michigan Attorney General after recent changes to Michigan's public-accommodation laws required the school to "lie" to students "by using pronouns inconsistent with biological sex," assign "sports teams" and "facilities" based on "gender identity" rather than sex, and refrain from explaining in a student handbook Catholic doctrines like those detailed in this book.[351] Queen of Angels Catholic Bookstore was compelled to sue the City of Jacksonville, Florida, over a public-accommodation law that "compels the bookstore to speak pronouns and titles based on its customers' 'gender identity' — thereby requiring the bookstore to prioritize self-professed identity over biological reality."[352] Jack Phillips — the owner of Masterpiece

---

[350] Ibid.

[351] Sacred Heart of Jesus Parish et al. v. Nessel, Western District of Michigan District Court, No. 1:22-cv-01214, Plaintiffs' Brief in Support of Their Preliminary Injunction Motive (December 22, 2022), 6–7; available at https://adflegal.org/sites/default/files/2022-12/Sacred-Heart-Of-Jesus-Parish-v-Nessel-2022-12-22-Plaintiffs-Memo-in-Support-of-MPI.pdf. https://perma.cc/U3QA-PU89

[352] The Catholic Store, Inc. d/b/a Queen of Angels Catholic Bookstore v. City of Jacksonville, Middle District of Florida District Court, No. 3:23-cv-00192, Plaintiff's Memorandum in Support of Motion for Preliminary Injunction (February 22, 2023), 1, https://adflegal.org/sites/default/files/2023-02/Queen-Of-Angels-v-Jacksonville-2022-02-22-Memo-In-Support-Of-MPI.pdf. https://perma.cc/K68T-AR3M

Cakeshop who won his case in the U.S. Supreme Court after respectfully declining to create a custom wedding cake that violated his religious beliefs — was immediately sued again by a gender activist under Colorado's public-accommodation law when the master baker respectfully declined to create a custom cake celebrating a "gender transition" that was requested immediately after the Supreme Court announced it would hear Jack's previous case.[353] The list continues to grow.

These examples show how government laws and policies are advancing an agenda that harms people of faith *and* those the government thinks it is protecting. They are the exact opposite of Church policies intended to promote human flourishing.

Government coercion

In chapter eight, we discussed the U.S. Department of Justice and the U.S. Department of Education's extraordinary "Dear Colleague" letter to the nation's schools. Recent actions taken by the federal government are no less aggressive. On his very first day in office, President Biden issued an executive order that purported to redefine "sex" under federal law to include "sexual orientation" and "gender identity."[354] Three weeks later, the U.S. Department of Housing and Urban Development issued a rule change. Under that Department's new policy, all colleges and universities in the United States — including religious colleges and universities, even those that accept *no* federal funding, under the theory that the federal government can prohibit discrimination in housing

---

[353] "Jack Phillips: Jack Is Back in Court, Again. Enough is Enough," *Alliance Defending Freedom*, https://adflegal.org/client/jack-phillips. https://perma.cc/R639-5T8L

[354] "Executive Order on Preventing and Combating Discrimination on the Basis of Gender Identity or Sexual Orientation," January 20, 2021, https://www.whitehouse.gov/briefing-room/presidential-actions/2021/01/20/executive-order-preventing-and-combating-discrimination-on-basis-of-gender-identity-or-sexual-orientation/. https://perma.cc/D8MH-4FAW

accommodations — are "forced to open their sex-specific dormitories, including dorm rooms and showers, to members of the opposite sex."[355] The policy has been challenged in court by the College of the Ozarks, a Christian school in Missouri that did not want to risk "ruinous financial penalties" if it continued to assign residence halls, communal bathrooms, and showers based on sex rather than "gender identity."[356]

In another Biden administration mandate, the U.S. Department of Health and Human Services requires "doctors to perform gender transition procedures on any patient, including a child, even if the procedure violates a doctor's medical judgment or religious beliefs." This directive prompted a lawsuit by the Catholic Medical Association and the American College of Pediatricians, who insist that under basic principles of medicine, "biological identity must remain the basis for treating patients." In their view, the department's mandate is "grossly overreaching its authority and, in so doing, putting children's psychological and physical health in great peril," setting "a dangerous precedent with incalculable implications for the ethical practice of medicine."[357] That dangerous mandate is paired with dangerous advice: President Biden's Department of Health and Human Services has issued a document describing what the federal government considers appropriate treatments for transgender adolescents, including " 'Top'

[355] "Implementation of Executive Order 13988 on the Enforcement of the Fair Housing Act," February 11, 2021, https://www.hud.gov/sites/dfiles/PA/documents/HUD_Memo_EO13988.pdf. https://perma.cc/YZ4X-X7MP

[356] Sarah Kramer, "College of the Ozarks Asks Supreme Court to Protect Its Freedom," *Alliance Defending Freedom*, May 19, 2021, https://adflegal.org/blog/meet-college-standing-biden-administration. https://perma.cc/U2DY-7VZW

[357] "Catholic Medical Association Joins Alliance Defending Freedom in Lawsuit Challenging Biden Transgender Mandate," *Catholic Medical Association*, August 26, 2021, https://www.cathmed.org/resources/catholic-medical-association-joins-alliance-defending-freedom-in-lawsuit-challenging-biden-transgender-mandate/. https://perma.cc/9AAV-RGC8

surgery — to create male-typical chest shape or enhance breasts" and "'Bottom' surgery — surgery on genitals or reproductive organs, facial feminization, or other procedures."[358]

Another lawsuit on behalf of Christian employers challenges the constitutionality of a Biden administration mandate requiring that religious nonprofit and for-profit employers fund "gender transition surgeries, procedures, counseling, and treatments" despite religious-based objections. The lawsuit alleges that the federal Equal Employment Opportunity Commission is misinterpreting federal sex-discrimination rules to demand that employers provide these medical coverages and procedures.[359]

In addition to these administrative maneuvers, members of Congress — supported by President Biden — introduced the cynically named "Equality Act."[360] The proposed legislation would add "sexual orientation" and "gender identity" as protected classes in many federal laws *without* any religious-liberty protections. In fact, the legislation *eliminates* existing religious-liberty protections under the Religious Freedom Restoration Act and other federal laws. If passed, government officials could use the law to violate the religious freedom of churches, religious organizations and schools, and everyday American citizens. The law could also be used to peel

[358] See "Gender-Affirming Care and Young People," *Office of Population Affairs*, https://opa.hhs.gov/sites/default/files/2022-03/gender-affirming-care-young-people-march-2022.pdf. https://perma.cc/N3H8-KGLL

[359] Mark Kellner, "Christian Employers Seek Injunction Against Biden Rule on Transgender Procedure Payments," *The Washington Times*, October 19, 2021, https://www.washingtontimes.com/news/2021/oct/19/christian-employers-seek-injunction-against-biden-/. https://perma.cc/FQG3-46WU

[360] "Statement by President Joseph R. Biden, Jr. on the Introduction of the Equality Act in Congress," *The White House Briefing Room*, February 19, 2021, https://www.whitehouse.gov/briefing-room/statements-releases/2021/02/19/statement-by-president-joseph-r-biden-jr-on-the-introduction-of-the-equality-act-in-congress/. https://perma.cc/K48N-8FVV

back protections for women in private spaces, like showers and locker rooms, and in athletic competition. Worse, the bill enshrines in federal law a definition of marriage and human sexuality that is directly at odds with the Catholic Church's teachings and detrimental to true flourishing and freedom.

Censorship

In chapter eight, we discussed the long journey of Walt Heyer, whose childhood trauma led to reassignment surgery from which he detransitioned eight years later.

Some years after detransitioning, Walt spoke on a Heritage Foundation panel at a Summit on Protecting Children from Sexualization. He told his story and truthfully testified:

> I stand before you with a mutilated body, with a life that was destroyed in many ways, redeemed by Christ certainly, but destroyed because I was affirmed and told how cute I look, how wonderful I was. And I went to a gender therapist who said, "All you need to do is have hormones and reassignment surgery."[361]

The panel presentation — including Walt's remarks — was posted on YouTube.

But YouTube took down the video. It said that Walt's words violated the company's hate speech policy, which "prohibits videos which assert that someone's sexuality or gender identity is a disease or mental illness." YouTube also said that Walt's viewpoint — that people are "not born transgender" — was unacceptable on its platform. YouTube did its part to censor an important

---

[361] Emily Jashinsky, "Exclusive: Man Tried to Share His Regrets about Transgender Life. YouTube Censored It," *The Federalist*, June 19, 2020, https://thefederalist. com/2020/06/19/exclusive-man-tried-to-share-his-regrets-about-transgender-life-youtube-censored-it/. https://perma.cc/DF7E-HFGU

conversation that directly impacts the physical and mental health and well-being of children.

We also discussed in chapter eight the story of Benji, who spent all her teenage years identifying as a transgender man. Benji's story also appeared in Abigail Shrier's *Irreversible Damage* book. The book's publisher, Regnery, sought to run a sponsored ad for the book on Amazon. While Amazon runs ads promoting the "transgender" agenda,[362] it would not allow Regnery's proposed ad. The expressed reason? "It contains elements that may not be appropriate for all audiences, which may include ad copy/book content that infers or claims to diagnose, treat, or question *sexual orientation.*" Keep in mind, the book is about a transgender epidemic among teen girls, not sexual orientation.[363]

But it wasn't just Amazon that objected to the message of *Irreversible Damage.* "Most major newspapers and trade magazines declined to review" Shrier's important book. "And when podcaster Joe Rogan hosted Shrier to discuss the book, employees at Spotify demanded that it take the interview off its platform." All of this was on top of social-media hate against Shrier, almost none of which "took issue with specific aims or arguments in her book" but "simply declared that the book was hateful, and that no decent human being should sell, buy or read it."[364]

[362] Abe Hamadeh, "Amazon's new transgender commercial targets children," March 19, 2023, https://twitter.com/AbrahamHamadeh/status/1637614425590087680. https://perma.cc/6R87-MRBK

[363] Abigail Shrier, "Amazon Enforces 'Trans' Orthodoxy," *Wall Street Journal,* June 22, 2020, https://www.wsj.com/articles/amazon-enforces-trans-orthodoxy-11592865818. https://perma.cc/G23C-EKWW

[364] Jonathan Zimmerman, "Commentary: Why Efforts to Censor Abigail Shrier's Book Will Backfire and Hurt Transgender People," *Chicago Tribune,* November 23, 2020, https://www.chicagotribune.com/opinion/commentary/ct-opinion-censorship-cancel-culture-abigail-shrier-transgender-20201123-sifw7khysrdpnbnj66qxp6yiam-story.html. https://perma.cc/3CJP-3CFP

As if that weren't enough, the American Booksellers Association issued a written apology to booksellers after the Association included Shrier's book in a promotional box with an ad sheet noting that more than sixty thousand copies of the book had been sold. In response to bookseller criticisms of the promotion, the Association apologized: "An anti-trans book was included in our July mailing to members," it said. "This is a serious, violent incident that goes against ABA's ends, policies, values, and everything we believe and support. It is inexcusable."[365]

Still, the offended booksellers said that wasn't good enough, so the Association issued additional apologies with increased smears against Shrier's carefully researched work. The Association's CEO issued a statement and said that the Association's promotion of Shrier's book was "egregious," "harmful," and "caused violence and pain." She described the promotional flyer as "negligent, irresponsible, and transphobic." The Association's board of directors added in an email to booksellers that the promotional "added to a toxic culture" and was "antithetical to the values [the Association is] working to promote." Despite all this, a member of the Association's Diversity, Equity, and Inclusion Committee was *still* critical of the Association and its leadership: "We're dealing with a historically white, cis [i.e., non-transgender] organization in a white supremacist society. So there are going to be a lot of missteps," he said. But he hoped the Association's "mistakes will provide instruction for booksellers around the country who also need to be more aware of pervasive discrimination against trans people and other marginalized groups."[366]

[365] Alex Green, "Booksellers Denounce ABA Promotion of Anti-Trans Book," *Publishers Weekly*, July 15, 2021, https://www.publishersweekly.com/pw/by-topic/industry-news/bookselling/article/86883-booksellers-denounce-aba-promotion-of-anti-trans-book.html. https://perma.cc/W2KR-5VR8

[366] Ibid.

Other books that tell the truth about gender ideology have also run afoul of Amazon. Earlier in this book, we referenced Ryan T. Anderson, who is President of the Ethics and Public Policy Center and the Founding Editor of *Public Discourse*, the Witherspoon Institute's online journal. Mr. Anderson's book, *When Harry Became Sally: Responding to the Transgender Moment*, was one of the first and most widely read books to question the gender-ideology movement. It is well-written and meticulously researched.

For years, the book was available on Amazon — until the weekend before Congress started debating the Equality Act, the aforementioned anti-religious legislation that seeks to impose gender ideology widely. Then Amazon removed Anderson's book from its platform so that it would not be available during the debate over the proposed Equality Act. In response to an inquiry from several U.S. Senators, Amazon claimed, falsely, that *When Harry Became Sally* framed "LGBTQ+ identity as a mental illness."[367] Given that Amazon controls over 70 percent of adult new-book sales and 80 percent of e-book sales, such censorship not only takes a book substantially out of the stream of commerce, but that censorship also makes it very difficult for publishers to justify printing new books in the subject area going forward — which means many books will never be written or published at all, no matter how much good the book might do for individuals struggling with their identity.

Public shaming

Martina Navratilova is one of the all-time greatest women's tennis players, having won nine Wimbledon singles championships and eighteen Grand Slam championships. She has also been a powerful spokesperson for the gay and lesbian lobby since coming out as same-sex attracted in

---

[367] Amazon Letter, March 11, 2021, https://s.wsj.net/public/resources/documents/Amazonletter0311.pdf. https://perma.cc/P5C4-P23V

1981. Yet in 2019, she lost her public platform — and her LGB support — "for publicly stating an obvious truth: Transgender women athletes have 'unfair physical advantages.'" In fact, Athlete Ally, a nonprofit with the goal of ending "rampant homophobia" in sports, chastised Navratilova as "transphobic," fired her as an Athlete Ally ambassador, and expelled her from the organization's advisory board.[368]

How did Navratilova find herself in such hot water? It started with a tweet expressing her view that "You can't just proclaim yourself a female and be able to compete against women." After heavy criticism of that comment, she decided not to speak about the subject until she had investigated it further. So she did. And then she wrote an op-ed for the *Sunday Times* of London. Here is what she said:

> I've [finished my research] and, if anything, my views have strengthened. To put the argument at its most basic: a man can decide to be female, take hormones if required by whatever sporting organisation is concerned, win everything in sight and perhaps earn a small fortune, and then reverse his decision and go back to making babies if he so desires. It's insane and it's cheating. I am happy to address a transgender woman in whatever form she prefers, but I would not be happy to compete against her. It would not be fair.
>
> Simply reducing hormone levels — the prescription most sports have adopted — does not solve the problem. A man builds up muscle and bone density, as well as a greater number of oxygen-carrying red blood cells, from childhood. Training increases the discrepancy. Indeed, if a male were to change gender in such a way as to eliminate any accumulated advantage, he would have to begin hormone treatment before puberty. For me, that is unthinkable....

---

[368] New York Post Editorial Board, "The Insane Gay Backlash against Martina Navratilova," *New York Post*, February 20, 2019, https://nypost.com/2019/02/20/the-insane-gay-backlash-against-martina-navratilova/. https://perma.cc/ZWV7-QA42

I also deplore what seems to be a growing tendency among transgender activists to denounce anyone who argues against them and to label them all as "transphobes." That's just another form of tyranny. I'm relatively tough and was able to stand up for myself in my Twitter exchange…, but I worry that others may be cowed into silence or submission.[369]

Athlete Ally then expelled Navratilova, opining that her "recent comments on trans athletes are transphobic, based on a false understanding of science and data, and perpetuate dangerous myths." An ACLU activist responded that "Athlete Ally's decision was absolutely, 100 percent correct." The U.K. *Independent's* chief sportswriter said that letting men identify as women and then winning every women's athletic championship would not be bad but "inspiring" for trans children or teenagers.[370]

A short while later, the BBC invited a spokesperson for the organization Fair Play for Women, a group that raises awareness and supports policies that protect the rights of women and girls in the U.K., to discuss Navratilova's opinions in a panel discussion with a trans athlete. That athlete — who identified as male until age twenty-nine but then claimed a female identity and medaled in a women's cycling world championship — refused to "participate in a discussion panel that takes [the organization] seriously and gives them a platform." So the BBC disinvited Fair Play for Women, and the athlete boasted about having the public media platform without opposing views. Dr.

[369] Martina Navratilova, "The Rules on Trans Athletes Reward Cheats and Punish the Innocent," *The Sunday Times of London*, February 17, 2019, https://www.thetimes.co.uk/article/the-rules-on-trans-athletes-reward-cheats-and-punish-the-innocent-klsrq6h3x. https://perma.cc/49E6-AX2V

[370] Madeleine Kearns, "In Defense of Women's Sports," *National Review*, February 27, 2019, https://www.nationalreview.com/2019/02/womens-sports-transgender-athletes-controversy-martina-navratilova/. https://perma.cc/FVE6-5V32

Nicola Williams, Fair Play's director and a research scientist with a specialization in human biology, was flabbergasted:

> Slurs (like "transphobia") get in the way of the collective good and the public are not hearing the full range of views.... Bully-boy tactics like this must be called out and not allowed to stifle the calm and rational discussion that's needed to find a resolution.[371]

But Navratilova's treatment was nothing compared to that of J. K. Rowling, the author of the wildly popular *Harry Potter* books and movies. Rowling's saga began with a tweet in December 2019 about Maya Forstater, who was terminated by a British think tank for tweeting her belief that biological sex cannot be changed but is immutable. While she says she affirms transgender individuals, Rowling could not endorse firing someone for resisting gender ideology. Rowling tweeted:

> Dress however you please.
> Call yourself whatever you like.
> Sleep with any consenting adult who'll have you.
> Live your best life in peace and security.
> But force women out of their jobs for stating that sex is real?
> #IStandWithMaya #ThisIsNotADrill[372]

The attack on Rowling was so loud and so fierce that it resulted in the *Vox* news site penning an article that wondered aloud whether Rowling had "just destroy[ed] the legacy of Harry Potter with a single, transphobic tweet."[373] Keep in mind that Rowling's *Harry*

---

[371] Ibid.

[372] Kyle Smith, "J. K. Rowling Indicted by Woke Enforcement Agency," *National Review*, December 19, 2019, https://www.nationalreview.com/corner/transgender-politics-vox-accused-j-k-rowling-of-transphobia/. https://perma.cc/TRV2-XAQY

[373] Ibid.

Potter books have "sold more than 500 million copies worldwide, making them the best-selling book series in history."[374]

As the public shaming intensified, Rowling decided to explain herself in a post on her own website; her essay is worth reading in its entirety.[375] She felt that an explanation of her stance was necessary after sharing a free children's book during the beginning of the COVID-19 pandemic and being met by a horde of online gender activists who accused Rowling of "hatred," called her "misogynistic slurs," and labeled her a "TERF," an acronym for "Trans-Exclusionary Radical Feminist," i.e., someone who believes that women cannot become men and men cannot become women. Rowling's lengthy essay was compassionate and well-supported by scientific evidence and stories. She knew it would result in more trouble, but she felt compelled to write it for the

> huge numbers of women [who] are justifiably terrified by the trans activists; I know this because so many have got in touch with me to tell their stories. They're afraid of doxxing [public dissemination of identifying information], of losing their jobs or their livelihoods, and of violence.[376]

Rowling didn't ask for sympathy or for agreement, simply that empathy and understanding "be extended to the many millions of women whose sole crime is wanting their concerns to be heard without receiving threats and abuse."[377]

[374] *Wikipedia, The Free Encyclopedia*, s.v. "Harry Potter," https://en.wikipedia.org/wiki/Harry_Potter. https://perma.cc/S6CN-NDKM

[375] J. K. Rowling, "J. K. Rowling Writes about Her Reasons for Speaking out on Sex and Gender Issues," *JKRowling.com*, June 10, 2020, https://www.jkrowling.com/opinions/j-k-rowling-writes-about-her-reasons-for-speaking-out-on-sex-and-gender-issues/. https://perma.cc/K3WB-Q36D

[376] Ibid.

[377] Ibid.

The response was immediate and ruthless. A *New York Times* writer implied that Rowling was responsible for increasing suicidal tendencies in gender-dysphoric people. A West Sussex school dropped its plan to name a dormitory building after her because it did "not wish to be associated with these views." Many former cast members in the *Harry Potter* movie series tweeted their condemnation and embarrassment. And an advisor to U.S. Senator Elizabeth Warren's campaign called Rowling "complete scum."[378]

Things continued to deteriorate, and by November 2021, Rowling returned to Twitter to share how she had been publicly shamed by gender activists. Noting that three activists posted pictures of themselves on Twitter standing in front of Rowling's house — "carefully positioning themselves to ensure that [her] address was visible" — Rowling reported that she had "now received so many death threats I could paper the house with them, and I haven't stopped speaking out." She continued, "Perhaps — and I'm just throwing this out there — the best way to prove your movement isn't a threat to women, is to stop stalking, harassing, and threatening us."[379]

When a society, and a culture, has lost its mind to this degree, there is only one appropriate loving response: to speak about God's plan for human sexuality with charity and truth. Yet knowing how and where to speak out can be challenging. And so we will conclude this book with a chapter that addresses the subject head-on, leaning heavily on Church officials and their advice about how to best respond in love to gender ideology.

---

[378] Madeleine Kearns, "J. K. Rowling vs. Woke Supremacy," *National Review*, June 12, 2020, https://www.nationalreview.com/2020/06/j-k-rowling-vs-woke-supremacy/. https://perma.cc/SY3N-WJQ2

[379] Madeleine Kearns, "J. K. Rowling Won't Back Down," *National Review*, November 22, 2021, https://www.nationalreview.com/corner/j-k-rowling-wont-back-down/. https://perma.cc/4MQ9-BQ3W

CHAPTER 10

How Do We Respond?

♀ ♂

AT THE LAST SUPPER, after He washed the disciples' feet, Jesus said, "A new commandment I give to you, that you love one another: just as I have loved you, you also are to love one another. By this all people will know that you are my disciples, if you have love for one another" (John 13:34–35). We are called to love one another as Christ loved us. As we explained earlier, this love entails willing the good of another, especially when others are experiencing difficulty and distress. That love is difficult and takes hard work, patience, and prayer.

Those who advocate for gender ideology claim that they support it in the name of love. But as previous chapters have demonstrated, gender ideology activists show their "love" by misleading parents and children, getting people fired, harassing and bullying those who speak the truth, sweeping scientific inquiry under the rug, and insisting that life-altering drugs and surgeries are the only path to happiness. There has to be a better way, a true and right way to love those who struggle with gender dysphoria and to correct those who think they are helping them.

Church leaders have taught extensively about the importance to human flourishing of speaking the truth and grounding our identity in God's love for us. This chapter will use these teachings to answer in detail common and difficult questions that confront Catholics living in a culture that espouses gender fluidity, questions such as: What should I do if my son or daughter announces that they are trans? How should I respond when someone demands that I refer to them with preferred pronouns and titles? Can Catholic health care professionals provide hormone blockers and cross-sex hormones? What should I do if my employer asks me to wear an LGBTQ "ally" pin? And so on. Whenever possible, the answers to these common questions will be direct quotations from source materials issued by Pope Francis and U.S. bishops.

What is the Catholic understanding of the human person?
Archbishop Robert J. Carlson:

> God made us male and female. God also made us a union of body and soul. God had a purpose and a plan in giving us the male or female body we have. How we live our masculine and feminine identity is certainly diverse, and there needs to be room for that. There's a wide variety of personalities, and they don't always fit gender-stereotypes. But ... being male or female is written into every cell of our body, and is part of the body-soul unity that we are.
>
> And that's the root issue. Gender ideology maintains that sex can be separated from gender. The Catholic understanding of the human person holds that sex and gender cannot be separated, and that there are limits to how we should manipulate our bodies. According to the Catholic understanding, there is, and is meant to be, a profound unity in the human person. "In fact it is from [one's] sex that the human person receives the characteristics which, on the biological, psychological and spiritual levels, make that person a

man or a woman, and thereby largely condition his or her progress towards maturity and insertion into society."[380]

Based on the unity of the human person, the basic challenge on this matter is articulated by the *Catechism of the Catholic Church* when it says: "Everyone, man and woman, should acknowledge and accept his sexual *identity*" [*CCC* 2333]. Long before gender ideology was a cultural topic, the *Catechism* had already named the central issue: this is a question of reconciling ourselves to the physical facts of sexual identity, not trying to change the facts according to how we think and feel.[381]

What does the Church mean by a body-soul unity?
Archbishop Jerome Edward Listecki:

The soul is the spiritual principle of each human person and the "subject of human consciousness and freedom." Yet man is truly himself only "when his body and soul are intimately united." The human person is not a soul or a mind that *has* a body merely as a biological accessory. Rather, the human person *is* a body formed by a soul. Human life and love are "always lived out in body and spirit," and thus the body is a "vital expression of our whole being." So integral, in fact, is the body to who we are as human beings that the body and soul *together* are fashioned and "destined to live forever." The [Nicene Creed] expresses a belief in the "resurrection of the body," or the belief that all persons will "rise again *with their own bodies* which they now bear." The body which will one day rise is the very body which each person received as a gift and in which each person lives out his vocation to holiness.[382]

---

[380] See Sacred Congregation for the Doctrine of the Faith, *Persona Humana* (Declaration on Certain Questions Concerning Sexual Ethics) (December 29, 1975), no. 1.

[381] Archbishop Carlson, *Compassion and Challenge*, 4.

[382] Archbishop Listecki, *Catechesis and Policy*, 2.1.

What is my identity?

Bishop John F. Doerfler:

> Human persons are created in the image and likeness of God. We are beloved sons and daughters of the Father. Jesus Christ died for us, which shows the depths of our human dignity.... We are not defined or identified by our sexual attractions or conflicts about sexual identity. Our fundamental identity is as a beloved son or daughter of God. Thus, it is best to avoid identifying persons merely using labels such as "gay" or "transgender." It speaks more to our fundamental identity and dignity as persons to speak of *persons* with same-sex attraction or *persons* with gender dysphoria.[383]

Pope Francis:

> "[Gender] ideology leads to educational programs and legislative enactments that promote a personal identity and emotional intimacy radically separated from the biological difference between male and female. Consequently, human identity becomes the choice of the individual, one which can also change over time." ... It needs to be emphasized that "biological sex and the socio-cultural role of sex (gender) can be distinguished but not separated."[384]

What are the philosophies behind gender ideology, and what is the Catholic response to them?

Archbishop Carlson:

> The philosophy underlying the movement seems to hold the following things:

[383] Bishop Doerfler, *Created in the Image and Likeness of God*, 5.
[384] Pope Francis, *Amoris Laetitia*, no. 56.

1. Feelings define our identity: "How you feel is who you are."

2. Human integrity means acting on our persistent desires. "I have to be true to myself."

3. Anyone who doesn't affirm our feelings and actions hates us.

As Catholics, we need to object to each of those ideas.

First, feelings are a *part* of us, but they do not *define* us. Thanks be to God they don't! As creatures who are both fallen and graced, we feel a lot of things every day. Following Jesus requires letting our identity guide our feelings, not the other way around....

Second, human integrity requires us to *sift* our desires, not simply *follow* them. I may want a dozen things before breakfast! We all do. But acting on every desire will lead to personal and social disintegration, not integrity.

The reason is simple: our desires have many sources. Some of them are rooted in our identity as God's sons and daughters. Some are the result of Original Sin.... For gender ideology, a feeling or desire is authentic and good if it is persistent, insistent, and consistent. But any number of examples can tell us that sinful and unhelpful desires — desires and feelings that are contrary to our identity as God's children, and lead us away from Heaven — can be persistent, insistent, and consistent. The persistent existence of a desire is no proof that "God made us this way." Sin and its effects are just as real as God's designs and grace when it comes to analyzing our human experience....

Third and last: disagreement is not hatred. Sometimes people object to our actions precisely because they love us. To love is to will the good of another. If I love someone, then sometimes I need to speak out. Parents, coaches, teachers, siblings, and friends can respect our freedom even while saying: "I don't think that's good for you. I don't see that bringing out the best in you."[385]

How should we treat those who identify as transgender?

Bishop Paul Coakley writes:

> Jesus commands us to love as we have been loved (John 13:34). Each person who identifies as transgendered is loved by God and is a person Jesus Christ died to redeem. To love like Christ means to desire the good of the individuals in our lives and to walk with them, regardless of their degree of openness to the good.[386]

Bishop Michael Francis Burbidge continues, explaining that a "disciple of Christ desires to love all people and to seek their good actively. Denigration or bullying of any person, including those struggling with gender dysphoria, is to be rejected as completely incompatible with the Gospel."[387] If the only thing you take away from this book is this — that those who oppose gender ideology believe that every single person must be treated as a child of God, made in His image and likeness, and is deserving of dignity, respect, and love — it will have been well worth your time.

At the same time, the purpose of this book is to demonstrate that treating someone with kindness and compassion *but without truth* — such as allowing a child to touch a hot stove — is not

---

[385] Archbishop Carlson, *Compassion and Challenge*, 6–7.

[386] Bishop Coakley, *On the Unity of the Body and Soul: Accompanying Those Experiencing Gender Dysphoria*, (April 30, 2023), 4–5, https://files.ecatholic.com/20256/documents/2023/5/On%20the%20Unity%20of%20the%20Body%20and%20Soul_Archbishop%20Paul%20Coakley_Pastoral%20Letter_English_2023.pdf?t=1682957274000. https://perma.cc/ZB7B-78H9

[387] Bishop Burbidge, *A Catechesis on the Human Person and Gender Ideology*, 4.

actually "love," because it does not will the good of the other. Bishop Burbidge goes on to address this point:

> In this sensitive area of identity … there is a great danger of a misguided charity and false compassion. In this regard, we must recall, "Only what is true can ultimately be pastoral."[388] Christians must always speak and act with both charity and truth. After the example of the Apostle Paul, they are to seek to speak the truth in love (see Eph. 4:15).[389]

Accordingly,

> when speaking with those who experience gender dysphoria or who claim a "transgender" identity, it is essential to listen and seek to understand their experiences. They need to know they are loved and valued, and the Church hears their concerns and takes them seriously. In every case, the person's dignity as a person beloved by God should be affirmed. Only in the context of an authentic dialogue will people be able to receive the truth, particularly truths that challenge their feelings or other beliefs.
>
> Special care must be taken when interacting with children who experience gender dysphoria or who express a belief in an identity incongruent with biological sex. Authentic accompaniment requires remaining firm in the truth of the human person while patiently guiding children towards that truth. Parents must always, and immediately, be involved in any discussions with a child about such sensitive topics.[390]

Finally, concludes Archbishop Carlson, "when someone you love is unhappy with their biological sex, listen! Keep the channels of communication

---

[388] See Congregation for the Doctrine of the Faith, *Letter to the Bishops of the Catholic Church on the Pastoral Care of Homosexual Persons*, no. 15.

[389] Bishop Burbidge, *A Catechesis on the Human Person and Gender Ideology*, 4.

[390] Ibid., 6.

open. We can sympathize with their feelings without [giving in] to their desires. It's important not to leave them feeling alone."[391]

Can I "affirm" someone's professed "gender identity" that is contrary to their sex?

No. To do so would be to affirm a lie, which is not willing the good of that person and therefore not loving.

Again, Bishop Burbidge:

> The claim to "be transgender" or the desire to seek "transition" rests on a mistaken view of the human person, rejects the body as a gift from God, and leads to grave harm. To affirm someone in an identity at odds with biological sex or to affirm a person's desired "transition" is to mislead that person. It involves speaking and interacting with that person in an untruthful manner. Although the law of gradualness[392] might prompt us to discern the best time to communicate the fullness of truth, in no circumstances can we confirm a person in error.[393]

Bishop Doerfler:

> Every one of us is created as either male or female. Thus, to live according to the truth of our human nature, we are to embrace our bodily sex. It is a gift given to us. Those who experience incongruence between their bodily sex and what they perceive their sex to be deserve our love, compassion, and care. A good analogy is how we would help persons who are suffering from anorexia nervosa. In this disorder there is an incongruence between how the persons perceive themselves and their bodily reality. They may perceive themselves as overweight when they are

---

[391] Archbishop Carlson, *Compassion and Challenge*, 11.

[392] See Pope St. John Paul II, *Familiaris Consortio* (November 22, 1981), no. 34.

[393] Bishop Burbidge, *A Catechesis on the Human Person & Gender Ideology*, 4.

quite thin. Just as we would refer a person with anorexia to an expert to help him or her, let us also refer persons with gender dysphoria to a qualified counselor to help them while we show them the depth of our love and friendship.[394]

Bishop Donald E. DeGrood:

> Material cooperation and scandal must be avoided. Pastors and school administrators are called to remain mindful that cooperation with individuals experiencing gender dysphoria can be viewed by the parish or school community as an implicit form of endorsement.[395]

But isn't affirmation merely a matter of manners and compassion?

No. As we have discussed, affirmation, at its core, is a lie that has the tendency to encourage others to embrace identities that are untrue and do not reflect reality, which harms the individual being affirmed. That shouldn't surprise us; as every parent appreciates, when we affirm a child's conduct and behaviors, we'll see more of that conduct and those behaviors, and when we do not affirm, we won't. That is why, as Bishop Burbidge explains:

> the acceptance and/or approval of a person's claimed transgender identity is particularly dangerous in the case of children, whose psychological development is both delicate and incomplete. First and foremost, a child needs to know the truth: He or she has been created male or female, forever. Affirming a child's distorted self-perception or supporting a child's desire to "be" someone other than the

---

[394] Bishop Doerfler, *Created in the Image and Likeness of God*, 6.
[395] Bishop DeGrood, *Diocesan Policy: Conforming with the Church's Teaching*, 5.

person (male or female) God created, gravely misleads and confuses the child about "who" he or she is.[396]

As is true in any situation, when we affirm someone's choices that stray from God's design, that is, when we affirm sin, there are consequences.

> "Gender-affirming" medical or surgical interventions cause significant, even irreparable, bodily harm to children and adolescents. These include the use of puberty blockers ... to arrest the natural psychological and physical development of a healthy child, cross-sex hormones to induce the development of opposite-sex, secondary sex characteristics, and surgery to remove an adolescent's healthy breasts, organs, and/or genitals. These kinds of interventions involve serious mutilations of the human body, and are morally unacceptable.[397]

Archbishop Carlson:

> Gender ideology asks us to conflate compassion and compromise. It says, in effect: "If you were compassionate, you would let me have my way."
> ... Gender ideology wants us to meet people where they are, capitulate to their demands, and celebrate them as they are. Jesus calls us to meet people where they are, proclaim the truth of God's plan, and accompany them along the way of that plan.

The bottom line is that "love always has two parts: compassion, and the challenging truth about God's plan. If we lack either — the compassion or the challenge — our love isn't fully Christian."[398]

---

[396] Bishop Burbidge, *A Catechesis on the Human Person and Gender Ideology*, 4.
[397] Ibid.
[398] Archbishop Carlson, *Compassion and Challenge*, 8, 12.

What about merely affirming pronouns?

Bishop Burbidge:

> The faithful should avoid using "gender-affirming" terms
> or pronouns that convey approval of or reinforce the per-
> son's rejection of the truth. It is not harsh or judgmental
> to decline to use such language. In the broader culture,
> Catholics may experience significant pressure to adopt
> culturally-approved terminology. However, in no circum-
> stances should anyone be compelled to use language
> contrary to the truth.[399]

Archbishop Carlson:

> The fundamental norm is that the biological sex of a per-
> son should provide the basis for all our interactions with
> them.... Clarity is not opposed to compassion. Clarity
> also comes from God's tender heart. Clarity needs to
> characterize our witness to the truth about the body.[400]

Bishop DeGrood:

> Whenever a class/schoolmate of a student experiencing
> gender dysphoria uses a pronoun that is inconsistent with
> the student's sex, this behavior shall be addressed imme-
> diately with instruction given to refrain from using the
> incorrect gender-specific pronoun.[401]

That means schools and businesses should not be forcing employees to affirm new pronouns either, right?

Correct. As Bishop Burbidge writes:

---

[399] Bishop Burbidge, *A Catechesis on the Human Person and Gender Ideology*, 5.
[400] Archbishop Carlson, *Compassion and Challenge*, 10.
[401] Bishop DeGrood, *Diocesan Policy: Conforming with the Church's Teaching*, 8.

The right to speak the truth inheres in the human person and cannot be taken away by any human institution. Attempts by the state, corporations, or employers to compel such language, particularly by threats of legal action or job loss, are unjust. We must love in the truth, and truth must be accurately conveyed by our words. At the same time, clarity must always be at the service of charity, as part of a broader desire to move people towards the fullness of the truth.[402]

How should I respond if my employer asks me to wear an LGBTQ "ally" pin or otherwise affirm ideas or behaviors at odds with Church teachings?

Sometimes employers will ask employees to show their commitment as "allies" to the LGBTQ movement by wearing apparel or taking some other action. That begs the question: allies to what? We can certainly be allies to the Church's teaching that everyone is created in the image and likeness of God and therefore worthy of dignity and respect. At the same time, we cannot be allies to an agenda that promotes ideas that are inconsistent with the Church's teachings, such as same-sex unions and gender ideology. Pope Francis provides some insight about how to approach this dilemma in his *Evangelii Gaudium*:

> Today, as the Church seeks to experience a profound missionary renewal, there is a kind of preaching which falls to each of us as a daily responsibility. It has to do with bringing the Gospel to the people we meet, whether they be our neighbors or complete strangers. This is the informal preaching which takes place in the middle of a conversation, something along the lines of

[402] Bishop Burbidge, *A Catechesis on the Human Person and Gender Ideology*, 5.

what a missionary does when visiting a home. Being a
disciple means being constantly ready to bring the love
of Jesus to others, and this can happen unexpectedly
and in any place: on the street, in a city square, during
work, on a journey. [403]

So we are called to preach the Gospel message to the extent possible,
even at work. Start a conversation and share your Catholic beliefs,
emphasizing that those beliefs are ordered to promoting flourishing
of every individual. At the same time, we are not required to cooper-
ate in activities that work against the Church, and we can request
reasonable religious accommodation as a matter of conscience when
an employer crosses that line.

What should I do if my employer tries to force me to choose between my faith and affirming gender ideology?

To begin, pray about the situation and discuss it with your priest or
spiritual advisor. See if there is a way to reach a compromise with your
employer without compromising your faith.

If a mutual agreement is not possible, you may need to seek legal
advice. You can turn to a local attorney experienced in religious-liberty matters or seek assistance from one of the many national public-
interest law firms that protect religious liberty such as Alliance
Defending Freedom, [404] Advocates for Faith and Freedom, the American Center for Law and Justice, Becket, First Liberty Institute, the
Great Lakes Justice Center, Liberty Counsel, the Thomas More Society, and the Thomas More Legal Center, among others.

---

[403] Pope Francis, *Evangelii Gaudium*, no. 127 (November 24, 2013), https://
www.vatican.va/content/francesco/en/apost_exhortations/documents/
papa-francesco_esortazione-ap_20131124_evangelii-gaudium.html.
https://perma.cc/2D2Y-XYLW

[404] See https://adflegal.org/request-legal-help. https://perma.cc/6UG8-Q3PS

But if we fail to affirm a professed trans identity, won't children commit suicide?

The idea that a child or teenager will commit suicide if his or her trans identity is denied is simply false. Bishop Burbidge writes:

> Although some advocates justify "gender affirmation" as necessary to reduce the risk of suicide, such measures appear to offer only temporary psychological relief, and suicidal risks remain significantly elevated following gender-transitioning measures....[405]
>
> Long-term studies show "higher rates of mortality, suicidal behavior and psychiatric morbidity in gender-transitioned individuals compared to the general population."[406] In addition, studies show that children and adolescents diagnosed with gender dysphoria have high rates of comorbid mental health disorders, such as depression or anxiety, are three to four times more likely to be on the autism spectrum, and are more likely to have suffered from adverse childhood events, including unresolved loss or trauma or abuse.[407] Psychotherapeutic treatments that incorporate "ongoing therapeutic work ... to address unresolved trauma and loss, the maintenance of subjective well-being and the development of the self," along with established treatments

[405] See Paul W. Hruz, "Deficiencies in Scientific Evidence for Medical Management of Gender Dysphoria," *The Linacre Quarterly* 87, no. 1 (February 2020): 34–42.

[406] See Juan Carlos d'Abrera et al., "Informed Consent and Childhood Gender Dysphoria: Emerging Complexities in Diagnosis and Treatment," *Australasian Psychiatry* 28, no. 5 (October 2020): 536–538; and Richard Bränström and John E. Pachankis, "Toward Rigorous Methodologies for Strengthening Causal Inference in the Association Between Gender-Affirming Care and Transgender Individuals' Mental Health: Response to Letters," *American Journal of Psychiatry* 177, no. 8 (August 2020): 769–772.

[407] See Kasia Kozlowska et al., "Australian Children and Adolescents with Gender Dysphoria: Clinical Presentations and Challenges Experienced by a Multidisciplinary Team and Gender Service," *Human Systems: Therapy, Culture, and Attachments* 1, no. 1 (February 2021).

addressing suicidal ideation are appropriate interventions.[408]
Gender transition is *not* the solution.

Indeed, to disregard or withhold information about
the harms of pursuing "transition" or about the benefits of
alternative, psychotherapeutic treatments constitutes a
failure in both justice and charity.[409]

Is the Church's teaching regarding transgender ideology consistent with scientific research?

Bishop Burbidge:

> We know from biology that a person's sex is genetically
> determined at conception and present in every cell of the
> body. Because the body tells us about ourselves, our bio-
> logical sex *does* in fact indicate our inalienable identity as
> male or female. Thus, so-called "transitioning" might
> change a person's appearance and physical traits (hor-
> mones, breasts, genitalia, etc.) but does not in fact change
> the truth of the person's identity as male or female, a truth
> reflected in every cell of the body. Indeed, no amount of
> "masculinizing" or "feminizing" hormones or surgery can
> make a man into a woman, or a woman into a man....[410]

How do I accompany someone struggling with gender dysphoria?

Bishop Doerfler:

---

[408] See Guido Giovanardi et al., "Attachment Patterns and Complex Trauma
in a Sample of Adults Diagnosed with Gender Dysphoria," *Frontiers in
Psychology* 9, no. 60 (February 2018).

[409] Bishop Burbidge, *A Catechesis on the Human Person and Gender Ideology*,
5; emphasis added.

[410] Bishop Burbidge, *A Catechesis on the Human Person and Gender Ideology*,
4. See also chapter four of this book.

Pastoral accompaniment [which is something all of us are called to do, not just members of the clergy] is the initial approach and subsequent establishment of an ongoing relationship of trust with another person to walk together on the path of conversion to follow Jesus Christ in faith.

Through the art of pastoral accompaniment, we meet people where they are and lead them step-by-step closer to Jesus Christ in a manner that is consistent with the Church's teaching.

Accompaniment requires patience. The path of conversion may take many years. For example, consider St. Monica's accompaniment of her son, St. Augustine [an accompaniment that took many, many years of prayer]. A common error is to force conversion according to a set timeline on another person.

In general, conversion and a change of behavior seldom happen in an instant. St. Augustine listened to the preaching of St. Ambrose for a considerable time before he finally had a change in heart and embraced a life of chastity. Thus, we must be patient and lead others step-by-step along the way....

To accompany others, it is insufficient merely to state the Church's teaching. In addition, we must strive to meet people and lead them, step-by-step, as we all walk toward the fullness of truth. Accompaniment requires docility to the Holy Spirt and discernment of the steps along the path. Discernment requires the virtue of pastoral prudence and must be carried out in fidelity to the teachings of the Church. Accompaniment does not dilute the teachings of the Church, but rather, animated by charity, we are to proclaim the Gospel in its fullness.

The path of accompaniment leads first to a deeper encounter with Jesus and a proclamation of the *kerygma* [the apostolic proclamation of salvation through Jesus Christ], the core message of the Gospel. In light of the experience of God's love and with the strength of his grace, people are then able to address sinful behavior. To address the behavior apart from fostering a personal encounter with Jesus and his love is likely to harm the other person. The grace of God makes conversion possible. Thus, we must begin the journey of pastoral accompaniment by striving to foster a personal encounter with Jesus Christ. Only then, can we shepherd people step-by-step to embrace and live the fullness of truth.[411]

Sr. Miriam James Heidland beautifully adds:

To admonish someone for their sins ... means to humbly and firmly warn, advise, or urge someone earnestly. It requires us to be very honest and forthright about our own lives, taking the log out of our own eye so we can see clearly to take the speck out of the other's eye (see Matt. 7:1–5). It means critically discerning with prayer and asking the Holy Spirt to open that person's heart and the timing of the encounter and to fill us with love and truth so that we can, when needed, humbly offer someone the gift of life and light. We offer the gift and surrender the rest to God, asking him to make up for any defect and to order that person's heart and ours as well. And then we pray (and even offer fasting) for that person.[412]

My child says that she or he is trans; what should I do?

Start with the Catholic Women's Forum at EPPC's *Person & Identity Project* website. The Project's "Parents" page provides basic information about gender ideology, frequently asked questions, parent resources, and a parent toolkit, including many informational documents that will

[411] Bishop Doerfler, *Created in the Image and Likeness of God*, 1–2.
[412] Sr. Miriam James Heidland, *Restore: A Guided Lent Journal for Prayer and Meditation* (Notre Dame, IN: Ave Maria Press, 2022), 137–38.

help you, your family members, and your parish priest work through the situation with love, compassion, and tenderness for your child.[413]

Among many valuable and critical resources, the Project includes a guide, published by the American College of Pediatricians, to finding a gender-ideology-critical therapist in your local area for a child with gender-identity distress.[414] It also provides a resource for finding Catholic counselors and support groups that will support your child in a way that is consistent with the Church's teachings about our identity, such as through Catholic Charities.[415] It provides links to support groups such as Parents of ROGD ("Rapid Onset Gender Dysphoria") Kids, Eden Invitation, and Sex Change Regret, and to sources of additional information, including the National Catholic Bioethics Center and the Society for Evidence-Based Gender Medicine. Parents of ROGD Kids also has an excellent guide to choosing a therapist for your child.[416] More resources are available through the Catholic Psychotherapists Association[417] and the National Catholic Bioethics Center.[418]

In addition, Bishop Burbidge adds:

> In difficult circumstances, parents are often tempted to think — or are made to feel — that their Catholic faith is at

[413] See https://personandidentity.com/parents. https://perma.cc/SPH7-AL2C

[414] See https://personandidentity.com/wp-content/uploads/2020/09/ACPEDS_Find_A_Therapist.pdf. https://perma.cc/6963-PE65

[415] See https://personandidentity.com/wp-content/uploads/2021/08/PIP-Counseling-and-Support-Groups.pdf. https://perma.cc/9LGQ-VX3U

[416] See https://www.parentsofrogdkids.com/therapists. https://perma.cc/7ZUQ-CH55

[417] See https://www.catholicpsychotherapy.org/resources/2022%20Conference%20Handouts/Integrating%20Body%20and%20Soul%20-%20Closing%20Plenary/Gender%20Dysphoria%20Resources.pdf. https://perma.cc/27RU-EQ4N

[418] See https://www.ncbcenter.org/resources-and-statements-cms/tag/Gender+Identity+and+Being+Transgender. https://perma.cc/SJ6W-ZABJ

odds with what is good for their child. In fact, authentic love for their children is always aligned with the truth. In the case of gender dysphoria, this means recognizing that happiness and peace will not be found in rejecting the truth of the human person and the human body. Thus parents must resist simplistic solutions presented by advocates of gender ideology and strive to discover and address the real reasons for their children's pain and unhappiness. [Parents] should seek out trustworthy clinicians for sound counsel. Meeting with other parents who have been through similar trials also can be a source of strength and support. Under no circumstances should parents seek "gender-affirming" therapy for their children, as it is fundamentally incompatible with the truth of the human person. Parents should not seek, encourage, or approve any counseling or medical procedures that would confirm mistaken understandings of human sexuality and identity, or lead to (often irreversible) bodily mutilation. Trusting God, parents need to be confident that a child's ultimate happiness lies in accepting the body as God's gift and discovering his or her true identity as a son or daughter of God.[419]

I think I might identify as a trans individual; what should I do?

Bishop Burbidge:

> Every one of us has a struggle that is unique. But none of us should feel alone or abandoned in his or her struggles. Like many others, you may feel alienated from your body, as though you are supposed to have a different one. Please know that, although you may struggle with your body or self-image, God's unrelenting love for you

---

[419] Bishop Burbidge, *A Catechesis on the Human Person and Gender Ideology*, 4, 6–7. See also chapter four of this book.

means that He loves you in the totality of your body as well. Our basic obligation to respect and care for the body comes from the fact that your body is part of the person — you — whom God loves.

Be on guard against simplistic solutions that promise relief from your struggles by the change of name, pronouns, or even the appearance of your body. There are many who have walked that path before you only to regret it. The difficult but more promising path to joy and peace is to work with a trusted counselor, therapist, priest, and/ or friend to come to an awareness of the goodness of your body and of your identity as male or female.

More than anything else, the Church desires to bring you the love of Jesus Christ Himself. That love is inseparable from the truth of who you are as one created in God's image, reborn as a child of God, and destined for His glory. Christ suffered for our sake, not to exempt us from all suffering but to be with us amid those struggles. The Church is here to assist and accompany you on this journey, so that you will know the beauty of the body and soul that God gave you and come to enjoy "the glorious freedom of the children of God" (Rom. 8:21).[420]

It is also critical that you pursue information and support immediately. Please see the resources listed in the answer to the previous question.

Is it ever acceptable to wear clothing associated with the opposite sex?

It depends. On the one hand, there are many overlapping cultural norms when it comes to clothing, and we must be careful not to rely on gross stereotypes of what a woman or man "should" wear. As covered earlier in this book, in the early 1900s, pink was the popular color for boys and blue for girls.

---

[420] Bishop Burbidge, *A Catechesis on the Human Person and Gender Ideology*, 7–8.

On the other hand, how we dress communicates to others something about ourselves, and we should never intentionally communicate a lie. It would be wrong, for example, if someone who has never served in the military or worked in a police department to wear military dress or a police uniform to mislead others into believing they are someone they are not. We must always communicate who we are in an authentic way, one that will lead to authentic relationships rather than relationships based on falsehoods. In a Catholic school "where a dress code or uniform exists," for example, all students should "follow the dress code or uniform that accords with their biological sex."[421]

The Catechism's teachings about modesty also provide helpful guidance:

> Purity requires *modesty*, an integral part of temperance. Modesty protects the intimate center of the person.... It guides how one looks at others and behaves toward them in conformity with the dignity of persons and their solidarity.... Modesty is decency. It inspires one's choice of clothing.... Modesty inspires a way of life which makes it possible to resist the allurements of fashion and the pressures of prevailing ideologies.
>
> The forms taken by modesty vary from one culture to another. Everywhere, however, modesty exists as an intuition of the spiritual dignity proper to man. It is born with the awakening consciousness of being a subject. Teaching modesty to children and adolescents means awakening in them respect for the human person.[422]

---

[421] Archbishop Listecki, *Catechesis and Policy*, 3.3.
[422] CCC 2521–24.

Should I be concerned about the influence of social media, television, and movies on my child?

The short answer is yes. As Bishop Burbidge writes:

> You [parents] are the first and the best teachers of your children. They will believe, pray, and love according to what they see, hear, and experience in your home. From you they will learn the truth of who they are, the dignity of the human body, the meaning of human sexuality, and the glory of their being children of God. *Nothing* can substitute for the school of the family. Still, you cannot fulfill this vocation by yourselves. The Church provides her teachings and pastoral care so that you can draw upon her wisdom and grace in teaching and caring for your children."[423]

As for social media, television, and movies:

> raising your children … requires vigilance against dangerous ideas and influences. This means the close monitoring of what your children receive via the internet and social media. Transgender ideology is being celebrated, promoted, and pushed out over all social media platforms and even children's programming. Much of your good work and witness can be undone quickly by a child's unsupervised or unrestricted internet access.[424]

Speaking as a parent rather than quoting from a representative of the Church, there are some commonsense steps you can take. Consider delaying buying your child a smart phone or tablet until they are at least fifteen, limit their amount of screen time per day, prohibit social media accounts unless absolutely necessary for school or after-school activities

---

[423] Bishop Burbidge, *A Catechesis on the Human Person and Gender Ideology*, 6; emphasis added.

[424] Ibid.

and then limit such accounts only for that use (e.g., monitoring practice times or receiving homework assignments). And when friends come to spend the evening or night, ask everyone to place their smart phone in a basket at the door where they can retrieve them on the way home. Your children may think you're unreasonable when they're teenagers; they will thank you when they're in their twenties.

Archbishop Carlson adds:

> Media treatments of transgender issues are full of double standards. Two consecutive stories in *Time* Magazine are a good illustration, and can stand for many other examples.
>
> The cover story from March 27 of 2017 ("Beyond He or She") celebrated the fact that, for today's generation of young people, gender is not determined by the physical facts but by how they feel about the facts. The very next cover story, from April 3 of 2017 ("Is Truth Dead?"), chided the president and claimed that, for him, the truth is not determined by the facts but by how he feels about the facts.
>
> Either the truth is determined by the facts or it is not. You can't have it both ways. To say that the truth is determined by the facts in one case and how we feel about the facts in another case is a double standard.[425]

Can I rely on my child's school to teach them about sex and gender?

Absolutely not. Bishop Burbidge writes:

> [A] strong source of misinformation about the nature of the person, and the meaning of the body is, regrettably, the public education system. Our ... public schools provide an excellent education in many regards. However,

---

[425] Archbishop Carlson, *Compassion and Challenge*, 7.

many also aggressively promote a false understanding of the human person in their advocacy of gender ideology. Current policies compel the use of chosen names and/or pronouns. Staff in many schools are required to affirm a child's declared "gender identity" and facilitate a child's "transition," even in the absence of parental notice or permission. Parents with children in public school [or even in private school or homeschool] must therefore discuss specific Catholic teaching on these issues with their children and be even more vigilant and vocal against this false and harmful ideology.[426]

How should a Catholic school respond to a child who identifies as transgender?

Bishop Doerfler:

> Students experiencing gender dysphoria are to be treated with compassion and respect. All unjust discrimination is to be avoided. Bullying of students must not be tolerated. Pastoral accompaniment is to be exercised to lead the student into a deeper union with the Blessed Trinity and to help them embrace and live according to the Church's teaching on sexuality.
>
> Students are to avoid behaviors associated with the attempt to redefine one's sex.
>
> Persons are to be addressed in accord with their legal name and pronouns corresponding to their biological sex.
>
> Bathrooms and locker rooms corresponding to one's biological sex are to be used. Consideration can be given to allowing [someone] to use a unisex bathroom.
>
> Students are to participate in sports according to their biological sex.[427]

[426] Bishop Burbidge, *A Catechesis on the Human Person and Gender Ideology*, 6.
[427] Bishop Doerfler, *Created in the Image and Likeness of God*, 10.

In addition, says Bishop Listecki, "where a dress code or uniform exists, all persons are to follow the dress code or uniform that accords with their biological sex."[428]

Can a person who identifies as transgender receive the sacraments of Baptism or Confirmation?

Bishop Doerfler:

> A person who publicly identifies as a different gender than his or her biological sex or has attempted "gender transitioning" may *not* be Baptized, Confirmed, or received into full communion in the Church, unless the person has repented. Repentance does not require reversing the physical changes to the body that the person has undergone. The experience of incongruence in one's sexual identity is not sinful if it does not arise from the person's free will, nor would it stand in the way of Christian initiation. However, deliberate, freely chosen, and manifest behaviors to redefine one's sex do constitute such an obstacle.[429]

Bishop DeGrood:

> Adults must accept the teachings of the Church when requesting Baptism for themselves. Those who are living a transgender lifestyle, considering transitioning, or undergoing transitions should be delayed until Church teachings are fully understood and professed as being accepted....
>
> [Regarding Confirmation,] those living a transgender lifestyle, considering transitioning, or have begun transitioning should be delayed until Church teachings are accepted.[430]

---

428 Archbishop Listecki, *Catechesis and Policy*, 3.3.
429 Bishop Doerfler, *Created in the Image and Likeness of God*, 7–8.
430 Bishop DeGrood, *Diocesan Policy: Conforming with the Church's Teaching*, 12.

Could that person serve as a sponsor to a sacrament?
Bishop Doerfler:

> A person who publicly identifies as a different gender than his or her biological sex or has attempted "gender transitioning" may not serve as a sponsor or a Christian witness for Baptism and Confirmation, unless the person has repented. Repentance does not require reversing the physical changes to the body that the person has undergone. The experience of incongruence in one's sexual identity is not sinful if it does not arise from the person's free will, nor would it stand in the way of the person serving as a sponsor of a Christian witness. However, deliberate, freely chosen, and manifest behaviors to redefine one's sex do constitute such an obstacle.[431]

How can we accompany someone who is prohibited from Baptism or Confirmation or from serving as a sponsor or witness of such a sacrament?
Pope Francis:

> If someone flaunts an objective sin as if it were part of the Christian ideal, or wants to impose something other than what the Church teaches, he or she can in no way presume to teach or preach to others; this is a case of something which separates from the community (see Matt. 18:17). Such a person needs to listen once more to the Gospel message and its call to conversion. Yet even for that person there can be some way of taking part in the life of community, whether in social service, prayer meetings, or another way that his or her own initiative, together with the discernment of the parish priest, may suggest.[432]

---

[431] Bishop Doerfler, *Created in the Image and Likeness of God*, 7.
[432] Pope Francis, *Amoris Laetitia*, no. 297.

Can someone who identifies as transgender receive Holy Communion?

Bishop Doerfler:

> Persons who identify as a different gender than their bio-
> logical sex or have attempted "gender transitioning"
> should not present themselves for Holy Communion.
> Pastors should address such situations privately with the
> persons and advise them that they should not present
> themselves for Holy Communion unless they have re-
> pented and received the Sacrament of Penance. Repen-
> tance does not require reversing the physical changes to
> the body that the person has undergone. The experience
> of incongruence in one's sexual identity is not sinful if it
> does not arise from the person's free will, nor would it
> stand in the way of the reception of Holy Communion.
> However, deliberate, freely chosen, and manifest behav-
> iors to redefine one's sex do constitute such an obstacle. If
> the behaviors are public and if the persons obstinately
> persist in such behaviors, they are not to be admitted to
> Holy Communion.[433]

Can someone who identifies as transgender serve as a liturgical minister or in a lay leadership role?

Bishop Doerfler:

> A person who publicly identifies as a different gender than his
> or her biological sex or has attempted "gender transitioning"
> may not exercise a liturgical ministry or position of leadership
> including but not limited to reader, extraordinary minister of
> Holy Communion, catechist, member of the parish finance or
> pastoral council, etc., unless the person has repented.

---

[433] Bishop Doerfler, *Created in the Image and Likeness of God*, 8, citing Catholic
Code of Canon Law nos. 915 and 916.

Repentance does not require reversing the physical changes to the body that the person has undergone. The experience of incongruence in one's sexual identity is not sinful if it does not arise from the person's free will, nor would it stand in the way of exercising a liturgical ministry or position of leadership. However, deliberate, freely chosen and manifest behaviors to redefine one's sex do constitute such an obstacle.[434]

Can a parish hold a funeral Mass for someone who identified as transgender?

Bishop DeGrood:

A funeral Mass may be offered for a deceased individual who professed his/her Catholic Baptism and who faced gender dysphoria in adulthood, even to the point of public expression of having been "transitioned." However, the funeral shall be prayed in a manner such that no endorsement that the individual "transitioned" is given by the Church and/or the priest celebrant. The individual's given/baptized name shall be used when referencing the deceased.

If the obituary written by the deceased/family members publicly endorses the false notion that he/she "transitioned," it shall not be permitted to be circulated at the liturgy. If a wake is to be prayed in the parish church, particular care is to be taken to ensure that any eulogy or public remarks made by mourners avoid giving public endorsements that the individual has "transitioned."

The Bishop shall be consulted by the priest celebrant on funeral plans in advance of the liturgy to ensure that public scandal, to the degree it can be avoided, is avoided in the praying of the funeral (CIC can. 1184 and 1185).[435]

---

[434] Bishop Doerfler, *Created in the Image and Likeness of God*, 9.
[435] Bishop DeGrood, *Diocesan Policy: Conforming with the Church's Teaching*, 13–14.

Does all this mean that someone who has taken steps to reject his or her sex is no longer welcome in the Church?

Absolutely not! As with anyone who walks away from the truth of the Church's teachings, the Church yearns for that person to repent and restore their broken relationship with Jesus Christ. While it is harmful to affirm or reject, it is loving to invite and accompany. Consider an analogy from Archbishop Carlson:

> The Church does not and cannot approve of abortion. After an abortion has taken place, however, the Church continues to care for the person. Healing ministries like Project Rachel and Project Joseph are an important part of the Church's approach to the issue of abortion. Similarly, the Church can and must continue to offer care to those who have taken irreparable steps to alter the sexual appearance and function of their body.[436]

And the Church must walk with that person as they attempt to detransition and claim their real identity as a daughter or son of God.

Don't the Church's teachings regarding gender ideology deny individual freedom?

No. In fact, the exact opposite is true. Archbishop Carlson writes:

> Gender ideology maintains that freedom is a matter of choosing, period. As Catholics, we understand freedom to be at once more noble and more nuanced than that.
>
> Human intellect is perfected by two things together: thinking and knowing the truth. Human intellect is most fully itself when it has both of these together. Catholic education has always, at its best, striven to perfect the intellect by building up both aspects.

---

[436] Archbishop Carlson, *Compassion and Challenge*, 12.

Something similar is true of human freedom. It's not perfected simply in choosing freely. We can all name examples of people freely choosing something that's bad for them and bad for others. Freedom is perfected in the combination of choosing freely and choosing the good.

A simple analogy comes from playing a musical instrument. You don't have more freedom simply because you've never had lessons. You're most free to make beautiful music when you've been trained and learned discipline. The same is true for excellence in human living.[437]

Can a Catholic hospital or health care facility provide hormone blockers or cross-sex hormones?

Archbishop Carlson:

> On the topic of Cross-Sex Hormones and Surgery…, the Church does not and cannot approve this. The national Catholic Bioethics Center has given excellent guidance which is worth citing at length:
>
> "Taking up or engaging in behavioral changes, including mannerisms, social cues, clothing, or modes of speaking that social mores ascribe to the opposite sex, does not alter the innate sexual identity of the embodied spirit, which is the human person. Hormonal interventions, to block the body's sex-specific hormones or provide the sex-specific hormones of the opposite sex, likewise alter nothing of a person's innate sexual identity…. So-called sex reassignment surgeries of any kind, designed to give the body an appearance with more of the culturally expected qualities of the opposite sex, also cannot modify the true sexual identity of the person, who was created male or female.

[437] Ibid., 7–8.

"Directly intending to transition one's given bodily sex into a 'new' one (even though this may be perceived as the 'real' and 'true' one) means intending to alter what is unalterable, to establish a false identity in place of one's true identity, and so to deny and contradict one's own authentic human existence as a male or female body-soul unity. Such an action cannot be consonant with the good of the whole person."

Hormonal and surgical interventions seem to promise hope. But it is, in the end, a false hope because it is not rooted in the truth about the body.... Catholic hospitals, physicians, and counselors ... [should] treat all patients and clients in accord with a genuine Catholic anthropology, with the understanding that anything contrary to Catholic teaching is not genuine care for the person.[438]

The Diocese of Springfield in Illinois explains that in these respects,

gender dysphoria can be reasonably compared to anorexia. Each is a condition in which a person, for a complex set of reasons, has a self-perception of his or her physical biology that is dislocated from reality. Just as it would be pastorally reckless to provide weight-loss resources to a visibly gaunt anorexic who thinks she is overweight, it is equally reckless to encourage someone with gender dysphoria to undergo hormone treatment and/or genital mutilation. None the less, the presentation of this truth must be made with love, compassion, and patience.[439]

[438] Ibid., 11–12.
[439] Diocese of Springfield in Illinois, "Pastoral Guide Regarding Policy § 650 Gender Identity," *Pastoral Guide Book Two: The People of God (Personnel Policies)* (January 13, 2020), 2; available at https://dio.org/wp-content/uploads/1667/43/Pastoral-Guide-and-650-Gender-Identity-Policy.pdf. https://perma.cc/28UM-YJDJ

That is why the USCCB reiterates unequivocally that "Catholic health care services must not perform interventions, whether surgical or chemical, that aim to transform the sexual characteristics of a human body into those of the opposite sex or take part in the development of such procedures." "Such interventions," the U.S. bishops continue, "do not respect the fundamental order of the human person as an intrinsic unity of body and soul, with a body that is sexually differentiated." Catholic health care institutions "must employ all appropriate resources to mitigate the suffering of those who struggle with gender incongruence, but the means used must respect the fundamental order of the human body."

"Only by using morally appropriate means," the bishops conclude, "do healthcare providers show full respect for the dignity of each human person."[440]

How should a Catholic politician respond to a proposed law that promotes transgender ideology?

The Congregation for the Doctrine of the Faith's *Some Considerations Concerning the Response to Legislative Proposals on the Non-Discrimination of Homosexual Persons* (1992) has valuable insights about politicians in the context of proposed legislation involving same-sex relationships that apply equally to this context:

> [Individuals who identify as transgender], as human persons, have the same rights as all persons including the right of not being treated in a manner which offends their personal dignity (cf. no. 10). Among other rights, all persons have the right to work, to housing, etc. Nevertheless, these rights are not absolute....

[440] USCCB Committee on Doctrine, *Doctrinal Note on the Moral Limits to Technological Manipulation of the Human Body* (March 20, 2023), 11–12; available at https://www.usccb.org/resources/Doctrinal%20Note%20 2023-03-20.pdf. https://perma.cc/S497-FFWD

Including [gender identity] among the considerations on the basis of which it is illegal to discriminate can
easily lead to regarding [gender identity] as a positive
source of human rights, for example, in respect to so-
called affirmative action or preferential treatment in hir-
ing practices. This is all the more deleterious since there
is no right to [gender identity] which therefore should
not form the basis for judicial claims. The passage from
the recognition of [gender identity] as a factor on which
basis it is illegal to discriminate can easily lead, if not automatically, to the legislative protection and promotion of
[gender identity]. A person's [gender identity] would be
invoked in opposition to alleged discrimination, and thus
the exercise of rights would be defended precisely via the
affirmation of the [transgender] condition instead of in
terms of a violation of basic human rights....

Since in the assessment of proposed legislation up-
permost concern should be given to the responsibility to
defend and promote family life (cf. no. 17), strict attention
should be paid to the single provisions of proposed measures. How would they affect adoption or foster care? ...

Finally, where a matter of the common good is concerned, it is inappropriate for Church authorities to endorse or remain neutral toward adverse legislation even if
it grants exceptions to Church organizations and institutions. The Church has the responsibility to promote family life and the public morality of the entire civil society
on the basis of fundamental moral values, not simply to
protect herself from the application of harmful laws....[441]

---

[441] CDF, *Some Considerations Concerning the Response to Legislative Proposals
on the Non-Discrimination of Homosexual Persons* (1992), nos. 12–16,
https://www.vatican.va/roman_curia/congregations/cfaith/documents/
rc_con_cfaith_doc_19920724_homosexual-persons_en.html. https://
perma.cc/AK43-9CWV

Should a Catholic institution give an honor that supports gender ideology, such as an honorary degree for a politician who endorses gender theory?

The USCCB's *Catholics in Political Life* (2004) states quite plainly:

> The Catholic community and Catholic institutions should *not honor* those who act in defiance of our fundamental moral principles.[442]

At what age should a parish youth program begin addressing the topic of sexual identity and the teachings of the Church?

The Catholic Women's Forum at the Ethics and Public Policy Center:

> Children naturally realize their sexual identity as they begin to take care of their bodies and learn the distinctions between boys and girls, brothers and sisters, mothers and fathers. As they grow older, discussions of modesty and chastity reinforce that distinction. Discussions of sexual difference should emphasize the equal dignity of males and females, while acknowledging differences. At the same time, acknowledging sexual difference should not enforce stereotypes or be interpreted to limit individual potential. Because gender ideology has saturated the culture, particularly public education, children are becoming familiar with — or even indoctrinated in — the basic tenets of gender ideology as early as kindergarten and elementary school. Parishes and dioceses should consider implementing their own policies on these issues,

---

[442] USCCB, *Catholics in Political Life* (2004), https://www.usccb.org/issues-and-action/faithful-citizenship/church-teaching/catholics-in-political-life https://perma.cc/3YTG-DKYA

with appropriate involvement of and deference to parents' authority and responsibility for their own children. In general, catechists should be trained and prepared to address questions related to LGBTQ issues and sexual identity, in age-appropriate and sensitive ways, when the issue is raised. For example, if a child mentions that a girl in her class "became" a boy, then the catechist might simply respond that even if a girl feels like she is a boy, or believes she is a boy, she is still a girl.

In middle school and high school, it is important to address these issues in the context of more comprehensive teaching about the human person and human sexuality. Some religious education programs have found that questions about sexual identity can be addressed, even indirectly, in classes that present the theology of the body, or through retreat programs that cover the person and sexual morality. Whenever parishes or dioceses implement programs addressing these issues for children and teens they might consider developing concurrent programs, or introductory presentations, for their parents as well.[443]

---

[443] The Person and Identity Project, "Questions and Answers for Parishes on Gender Ideology" (2021), 3–4, https://personandidentity.com/wp-content/uploads/2021/08/PIP-Parish-FAQs-Download-2021.pdf. https://perma.cc/5RS6-AW58

Conclusion

♀ ♂

I HOPE THAT THIS book is merely the beginning of your journey toward exploring the beautiful truths that the Catholic Church teaches regarding marriage and human sexuality. In the following section, I've recommended some additional resources for further study. In addition, the pope, our bishops, and many Catholic theologians and authors are constantly adding new insights to help us continue to grow closer to God, discern His will, and keep our hope in Him. To that end, here are a few closing thoughts.

First, God loves us. He cares for us, and He wants us to flourish in this life and spend eternity with Him in the next. What's more, because He made us, God knows what we must do to accomplish those ends. He guides us with the instruction book of the Scriptures and apostolic tradition as manifested in the Catholic Church's teaching authority. When we follow His plan, we thrive as human beings.

Second, God's plan has very specific teachings and directions about how we are to use our bodies and our sexuality. Each of us is a body-soul unity, intentionally created by God as male or female, and our sex informs who we are and how we relate to others. Our sexuality is a gift and something to be freely given only to our spouse within the confines of a sacramental marriage in the Church, and without conditions or the holding back of any part of ourselves. When we follow God's plan, we become co-creators with God of new life, and our families serve as an icon of the Holy Trinity to others.

Third, because God loves us, He does not force us to follow His guidance. If we want to do things our own way and ignore God's way, He gives us free will to make that choice. But when we reject God's plan for our lives and follow our own desires and ends, we invite a life of challenge and heartache not only for ourselves but for our families, friends, and the many other people whose lives we touch.

Fourth, we cannot give in to peer pressure or cultural expectations that violate the Word of God. We must continue to proclaim the good news of Jesus Christ with the help of the Catholic Church's teachings. When we encounter others who struggle with their sexual identity, our first response must *always* be compassion, care, and pastoral accompaniment. And that response must be grounded in the truth about sexuality and human flourishing. Relationships built on compassion, respect, and sensitivity but not truth will inevitably collapse, hurting our brothers and sisters in need and wounding us as well. It is far better to proclaim the truth today than someday to be faced with the anguished question from a detransitioner: "Why didn't you tell me?"

Fifth, the cultural push for gender ideology may seem new and difficult to understand, an almost insurmountable challenge to the way we try to live our faith in the world. But as G. K. Chesterton once wrote:

> nine out of ten of what we call new ideas are simply old mistakes. The Catholic church has for one of her chief duties that of preventing people from making those old

mistakes; from making them over and over again forever, as people always do if they are left to themselves.[444]

Chesterton's admonition certainly holds in this context: gender activists are pushing for the same philosophical separation of body and soul that was championed by Gnostic heretics in the second century and by many others in the ages since. In other words, we keep our hope in Christ knowing that the Church has been down this road before, and that God is never "surprised" by the creative ways that humans try to thwart His heavenly design.

Sixth, the Catholic Church's teachings about marriage and human sexuality might seem difficult. But God gives us the grace to live by them, and there are rich blessings that come from following them and rejecting the many contrary messages we hear from our modern culture: that there is no such thing as objective truth, that we should act on our feelings and not out of reason and discipline, that we should pursue personal gratification at any cost, and that we cannot trust that there is an eternal God who loves us and always wants what is best for us. Not coincidentally, these are the very same lies the serpent told Adam and Eve in the Garden of Eden. Satan has been using them against us ever since.

Finally, the demands of our Creator are modest: to love and trust Him completely, to love our neighbors as ourselves, and to work with God to advance His Kingdom here on earth. We do not need to solve the problem of culture's obsession with gender ideology; nor are we responsible for changing someone's mind about the subject. Like the boy in John 6:9 who offered Christ all that he had — five barley loaves and two fish — all we need to do is to take our meager gifts and give them to the Lord. He will do the rest.

---

[444] G. K. Chesterton, "Why I Am a Catholic," from *Twelve Modern Apostles and Their Creeds* (1926), reprinted in *The Collected Works of G. K. Chesterton*, vol. 3 (San Francisco: Ignatius Press, 1990); available at https://www.chesterton.org/why-i-am-a-catholic/. https://perma.cc/PJ4H-U34Q

Additional Resources

♀ ♂

THIS BOOK MAY BE the first in-depth resource you have read about gender ideology, or it may the latest of many. Either way, knowing how to respond to gender ideology is both complicated and important, and there is much more to learn. Consider the following resources, many of which have been referenced in this book:

The Catholic Women's Forum at the Ethics and Public Policy Center's *Person and Identity Project* website, personandidentity. com. The Project offers formation, workshops, and pastoral guidance on transgender issues and the human person, and its website includes a plethora of resources for parents, schools, churches, and medical professionals.

The Catholic Diocese of Arlington, *A Catechesis on the Human Person and Gender Ideology* (August 12, 2021), available at https://www.arlingtondiocese.org/Communications/Bishop/ Public-Messages/A-Catechesis-on-the-Human-Person-and-

Gender-Ideology-Catholic-Diocese-of-Arlington.pdf. https://
perma.cc/F57Q-FUU5

The Catholic Diocese of Marquette, *Created in the Image and
Likeness of God: An Instruction on Some Aspects of the Pastoral
Care of Persons with Same-Sex Attraction and Gender Dysphoria*
(July 29, 2021), available at https://dioceseofmarquette.org/
pastoral-messages-instructions-and-resources. https://perma.
cc/T54U-RS36

The Catholic Archdiocese of St. Louis, *Compassion and Challenge:
Reflections on Gender Ideology from Archbishop Robert J. Carlson*
(June 1, 2020), available at https://www.archstl.org/Portals/0/
Pastoral%20letters/Compassion%20and%20Challenge%20-%20
letter%20size.pdf. https://perma.cc/74QQ-JD9Y

The Catholic Diocese of Lansing, *Theological Guide: The Human
Person and Gender Dysphoria* (January 15, 2021), available at
https://www.flipsnack.com/dolmi/theological-guide-the-
human-person-and-gender-dysphoria.html. https://perma.
cc/3GNG-29FH

The Catholic Archdiocese of Oklahoma City, *On the Unity of the
Body and Soul: Accompanying Those Experiencing Gender
Dysphoria* (April 30, 2023), available at https://files.ecatholic.
com/20256/documents/2023/5/On%20the%20Unity%20
of%20the%20Body%20and%20Soul_Archbishop%20Paul%20
Coakley_Pastoral%20Letter_English_2023.
pdf?t=1682957274000. https://perma.cc/UA53-WA5L

Congregation for Catholic Education, *Male and Female He Created
Them: Towards a Path of Dialogue on the Question of Gender
Theory in Education* (2019), available at http://www.educatio.
va/content/dam/cec/Documenti/19_0997_INGLESE.pdf.
https://perma.cc/3VHR-5JWF

Ryan T. Anderson, *When Harry Became Sally: Responding to the Transgender Moment* (New York: Encounter Books, 2018). This is not a religious book, but it does an excellent job discussing the nature and science of personhood.

Abigail Shrier, *Irreversible Damage: The Transgender Craze Seducing Our Daughters* (Washington, DC: Regnery Publishing, 2020). This is also not a religious book, but it does an excellent job discussing gender identity as a social contagion.

Christopher West, *Theology of the Body for Beginners: A Basic Introduction to Pope John Paul II's Sexual Revolution* (West Chester, PA: Ascension Press, 2009). An excellent introduction and summary of Pope St. John Paul II's extraordinary theology about how the human body helps us understand God.

Emily Stimpson, *These Beautiful Bones: An Everyday Theology of the Body* (Steubenville, OH: Emmaus Road Publishing, 2013). Emily has a beautiful way of talking about the Theology of the Body.

Edward Sri, *Who Am I to Judge?: Responding to Relativism with Logic and Love* (San Francisco: Ignatius Press, 2016). An absolute must-read book about moral relativism, virtue, and the classical moral worldview.

Fr. Michael Schmitz, *Made for Love: Same-Sex Attraction and the Catholic Church* (San Francisco: Ignatius Press, 2017). This is an outstanding book for many reasons, but I direct you especially to chapter seven, regarding identity.

Acknowledgments

♀ ♂

A SPECIAL THANKS TO Drs. Miriam Grossman, Michael Laidlaw, Quentin Van Meter, and Andre Van Mol, who compiled many of the resources in chapters four and six to submit legal briefs on these issues in conjunction with my work at Alliance Defending Freedom.

I also greatly appreciate the contributions of my exceptionally talented editors at Sophia Institute Press, Drew Oliver and Laura Bement; of Dr. Lesley Rice, Assistant Professor of Bioethics at the Pontifical John Paull II Institute for Studies on Marriage & Family at the Catholic University of America; and of my wife, professional colleagues, and family members who reviewed early drafts of this book. All of them were indispensable to the final product.

Finally, thank you to Dr. David Crawford for his time and care in reviewing this book for the *Nihil Obstat* and to Bishop Walkowiak for issuing his *Imprimatur*. I am deeply indebted to both of them.

Appendix 1: On Virtue

♀ ♂

THE *CATECHISM* DESCRIBES FOUR cardinal (central, or prime) virtues. Prudence "disposes practical reason to discern our true good in every circumstance and to choose the right means of achieving it." Justice disposes us "to respect the rights of each and to establish in human relationship the harmony that promotes equity with regard to persons and to the common good." Fortitude "strengthens the resolve to resist temptations and to overcome obstacles in the moral life." And temperance "moderates the attraction of pleasures and provides balance in the use of created goods" (*CCC* 1806–1809).

The *Catechism* goes on to identify three theological virtues. Faith is the "virtue by which we believe in God and believe all that he has said and revealed to us, and that Holy Church proposes for our belief, because he is truth itself." Hope is the "virtue by which we desire the kingdom of heaven and eternal life as our happiness, placing our trust in Christ's promises and relying not on our own strength, but on the help of the grace of the Holy Spirit.... Buoyed up by hope," we are "preserved from selfishness and led to the happiness that flows from charity." Charity is the "virtue by which we love God above all things for his own sake, and our neighbor as ourselves for the love of God" (*CCC* 1814, 1817, 1818, 1822).

The virtues are relational skills that allow us to live the two greatest commandments: love God and love our neighbor. As Catholic theologian Edward Sri explains it:

> If I lack in the virtue of generosity, I will do selfish things that hurt my spouse. If I lack prudence and spend too many hours preoccupied with work, my kids will feel the effects of the imprudent way I use my time. If I often get overwhelmed with life and become easily irritated, the people in my life will suffer the effects of my lack of patience and perseverance.[445]

So how do we obtain the virtues? Like any other habit: practice.

If I decide I want to be an NFL quarterback (or even a college football coach) but I take no actions to achieve that goal, I will never make those dreams a reality, no matter how big and fast I am. I need to practice passing. Reading defenses. Avoiding tackles. Executing an offensive playbook. And developing leadership skills and learning how to inspire those around me.

The same is true with our relationships with God and each other. The skills we need to develop those relationships are known as "the virtues," the "habitual and firm disposition to do the good." They allow us "not only to perform good acts, but to give the best of" ourselves (*CCC* 1803).

Start by identifying one way in which your skill to do good is lacking. Perhaps it is a lack of prudence in the way you talk about others when they are not present — in other words, you are prone to gossip. Then study the lives of saints who were successful in building

---

[445] Sri, *Who Am I to Judge?*, 44.

others up rather than tearing them down. Figure out how you can model that conduct. For example, the next time you are in a conversation and talking about someone else, find a way to say something positive about that person to make him or her appear in a good light. When a negative thought creeps into your mind, bite your tongue. Pray to God and ask Him to give you the grace to have prudence in your conversations about others, especially when you have received the Eucharist. And make frequent use of Confession when you fall short of the standard to which God is calling you.

One of the best places to practice virtue is in your family. The family is a gymnasium for "exercising" virtue. Choosing to put others' interests before ourselves, remaining steadfast in our faith when things do not go our way, placing our trust in Christ when a family member hurts us (even unintentionally): these are concrete situations for us to practice the skills that we want to define all our relationships.

Dr. Tim Gray, President of the Augustine Institute, has referred to the family as a holiness machine. Living and interacting with family members in the give-and-take of everyday work, school, and family life results in friction and the sanding down of our rough edges: the kind of slow, long-term change that helps us grow in virtue and holiness.

Appendix 2: On Science and Religion

As MANY AS 70 percent of Catholic emerging adults in America believe the lie that scientific knowledge and religious faith are in sharp conflict.[446] Criticism of the Church with respect to scientific inquiry can be traced back to at least the time of Galileo, when the Church was misunderstood and maligned regarding its dialogue with the scientific community. As history continued into the modern age, the lie concerning the supposed conflict between faith and science only deepened.

By the 1800s, and as a result of the individualistic philosophies being promoted by so-called Enlightenment philosophers, a suspicion of Christian doctrines (other than moral teachings) arose among the intellectual class. Such critics, especially Protestant, Deist, and agnostic scholars, began to use common Church terms,

[446] Christopher Baglow, "A Catholic History of the Fake Conflict Between Science and Religion," *University of Notre Dame: Church Life Journal,* May 4, 2020, https://churchlifejournal.nd.edu/articles/a-catholic-history-of-the-conflict-between-religion-and-science/. https://perma.cc/4SJ4-WHC8

including "dogma," "divine mystery," and "articles of faith," to imply foolishness, fear of human progress, and deception. Consider an 1816 letter that Thomas Jefferson, a Deist, wrote to a friend about the dogma of the Trinity:

> Ridicule is the only weapon which can be used against unintelligible propositions. Ideas must be distinct before reason can act upon them; and no man ever had a distinct idea of the trinity. It is the mere Abracadabra of the [tricksters] calling themselves the priests of Jesus.[447]

By the late 1800s, some saw Church dogmas only as irrational statements of faith that required correction by scientific study."[448] These critics failed to recognize that the Church has always been a leader in the field of scientific inquiry — from Copernicus to Fr. Gregor Mendel and from Louis Pasteur to Fr. Georges Lemaître — and ignored that Church dogmas are reached only through intense study, investigation, and rational reasoning.

Indeed, before the 1800s, the term "science" (from the Latin word *scientia*, which means "knowledge") meant any knowledge demonstrated through logic, including theology.[449] But during the 1800s, terms like "science" and "scientific method" began to be used only with the study of our physical universe through experiment and observation, leaving the misimpression that other fields of knowledge and rational thought, such as theology but also including art, philosophy, and morality, were unserious and not worthy of study.[450]

---

[447] Thomas Jefferson to Francis Adrian Van der Kemp, July 30, 1816; available at https://founders.archives.gov/documents/Jefferson/03-10-02-0167. https://perma.cc/C6BD-W2XQ

[448] Baglow, "A Catholic History of the Fake Conflict Between Science and Religion."

[449] Ibid., emphasis added.

[450] Ibid.

This cultural transformation was joined in the United States by a xenophobic anti-Catholic prejudice that feared Catholics wanted the pope to control the country. As a result, the public associated science with progress and Catholicism with superstition, allowing false claims about the Church's rejection of science to abound.[451]

These trends culminated in John William Draper's 1874 publication of his influential book, *History of the Conflict Between Religion and Science*. Based on little or no evidence, Draper presented a stark — and false — conflict between science and Catholicism. A later collection of essays, *Galileo Goes to Jail and Other Myths about Science and Religion*, debunked many of Draper's claims. Yet Draper's book was so popular that it has now been translated into ten languages and been reprinted fifty times.[452]

To be clear, the Church does not pit dogmas, the Bible, the *Catechism of the Catholic Church*, or any other Catholic teaching against scientific inquiry. Quite the opposite! The Church teaches that God created the physical world, and because the Church also teaches that God is rational, divine revelation and reason must always align. That is why numerous great scientists were Catholic, including lay people such as Galileo, Pascal, Ampère, de Fermat, Cauchy, and Christian Doppler, and clergy, including Fr. Roger Bacon, Grimaldi, William of Ockham, and too many more to list here. However, the Church does recognize that there are realms of knowledge — from fundamental questions like "Why is there something rather than nothing?" to the definitions of beauty and goodness and truth — that the scientific method is, in its nature, incapable of addressing.

Again, it is Pope St. John Paul II who helps us understand the relationship between Church teaching and what we now call science. In a June 1, 1988 letter to Fr. George Coyne, S.J., the Director of the

[451] Ibid.
[452] Ibid.

Vatican Observatory, one of the oldest astronomical research institutions in the world, he described it this way:

> The unity that we seek … is not identity. The Church does not propose that science should become religion or religion science. On the contrary, unity always presupposes the diversity and the integrity of its elements. Each of these members should become not less itself but more itself in a dynamic interchange, for a unity in which one of the elements is reduced to the other is destructive, false in its promises of harmony, and ruinous of the integrity of its components. We are asked to become one. We are not asked to become each other.[453]

In this way, scientific inquiry and religion become partners, reinforcing and improving the knowledge of the other. Pope St. John Paul II continues:

> Science can purify religion from error and superstition; religion can purify science from idolatry and false absolutes. Each can draw the other into a wider world, a world in which both can flourish.
>
> For the truth of the matter is that the Church and the scientific community will inevitably interact; their options do not include isolation. Christians will inevitably assimilate the prevailing ideas about the world, and today these are deeply shaped by science. The only question is whether they will do this critically or unreflectively, with depth and nuance or with a shallowness that debases the Gospel and leaves us ashamed before history. Scientists, like all human beings, will make decisions upon what ultimately gives meaning and value to their lives and to their work. This they will do well or poorly, with the reflective

---

[453] Pope St. John Paul II, "Letter to Reverend George V. Coyne, S.J., Director of the Vatican Observatory."

depth that theological wisdom can help them attain, or with an unconsidered absolutizing of their results beyond their reasonable and proper limits....

Only a dynamic relationship between theology and science can reveal those limits which support the integrity of either discipline, so that theology does not profess a pseudo-science and science does not become an unconscious theology.... The uses of science have on more than one occasion proved massively destructive, and the reflections on religion have too often been sterile. We need each other to be what we must be, what we are called to be.[454]

These principles apply to what the sciences have to say about gender ideology just as much as they do any other field. And as in other fields, Church teaching and the scientific evidence regarding "gender identity" do not conflict but are harmonious.

[454] Ibid.

About the Author

JOHN J. BURSCH SERVES as vice president of appellate advocacy for Alliance Defending Freedom (ADF), the largest public-interest law firm in the world defending religious liberty, free speech, parental rights, marriage and family, and the right to life. John has argued twelve cases in the U.S. Supreme Court, including cases defending the Catholic Church's teachings on marriage and sexuality. John speaks frequently to groups — both religious and secular — about topics including marriage, human sexuality, the right to life, and religious liberty. A married father of five, John is a Fourth Degree Knight of Columbus, a three-time past president of the Grand Rapids Legatus Chapter, and a member of the Pro-Life Partners Foundation Advisory Board. The thoughts expressed in this book do not purport to reflect those of ADF or its clients.

Sophia Institute

Sophia Institute is a nonprofit institution that seeks to nurture the spiritual, moral, and cultural life of souls and to spread the Gospel of Christ in conformity with the authentic teachings of the Roman Catholic Church.

Sophia Institute Press fulfills this mission by offering translations, reprints, and new publications that afford readers a rich source of the enduring wisdom of mankind.

Sophia Institute also operates the popular online Catholic resource CatholicExchange.com. *Catholic Exchange* provides world news from a Catholic perspective as well as daily devotionals and articles that will help readers to grow in holiness and live a life consistent with the teachings of the Church.

In 2013, Sophia Institute launched Sophia Institute for Teachers to renew and rebuild Catholic culture through service to Catholic education. With the goal of nurturing the spiritual, moral, and cultural life of souls, and an abiding respect for the role and work of teachers, we strive to provide materials and programs that are at once enlightening to the mind and ennobling to the heart; faithful and complete, as well as useful and practical.

Sophia Institute gratefully recognizes the Solidarity Association for preserving and encouraging the growth of our apostolate over the course of many years. Without their generous and timely support, this book would not be in your hands.

www.SophiaInstitute.com
www.CatholicExchange.com
www.SophiaInstituteforTeachers.org

Sophia Institute Press˙ is a registered trademark of Sophia Institute.
Sophia Institute is a tax-exempt institution as defined by the
Internal Revenue Code, Section 501(c)(3). Tax I.D. 22-2548708.